The Gospel of the Kingdom

Endorsements

My friend, Greg Hood, is not only a teacher of the Word, but he is a student. Ever learning, ever maturing...as we all should be. The concepts and truth in this book may be new to you and that's okay. They are based on Scripture yet are just coming into their season. Kingdom, Kingdom Connection, Ekklesia, Apostles, Reigning in Life and so much more within these pages that will inspire you and encourage you and above all, change you. I encourage you to grab a cup of coffee, open your hearts and minds to what God is saying and doing, and take notes! Get ready to grow.

Tim Sheets, Apostle
Author of *Angel Armies, Angel Armies on Assignment, Planting the Heavens*
Tim Sheets Ministries
The Oasis Church, Middletown, Ohio
www.timsheets.org

In *The Gospel of the Kingdom,* my friend Greg Hood gives us language that stirs our hearts with a fresh passion to see God's governmental rule manifested in the earth. This book will help develop in you a heart for that which God Himself is passionate about. Let it stir you with that which stirs Him, the redemption of all things back to Himself.

Robert Henderson
Best-Selling Author, *Courts of Heaven Series*

The Gospel of the Kingdom will revolutionize how believers live out the mission and mandate of Christ to change our world. Apostle Greg

Hood brings a fresh approach to this vital topic which will empower members of Christ's Ekklesia to use their God given authority to cause God's Kingdom to come & will to be done on earth as it is in heaven.

Jane Hamon, Apostle
Vision Church
Author of *Dreams & Visions, The Deborah Company, Discernment and Declarations for Breakthrough*

Apostolic and Prophetic voices everywhere agree that the church, the ekklesia, has shifted into a new age, a new Reformation. In his book, *The Gospel of the Kingdom*, Dr. Greg Hood challenges believers to shift out of a mindset of practicing a religion into one of fulfilling God's original Kingdom mandate to redeem and restore the earth. As God's earthly ambassadors of His Kingdom, we must grasp the authority and responsibility invested in us, and to examine scripture in a fresh light and understanding so that we can cause the kingdoms of this world to become the kingdoms of our Lord and of his Christ.

Tom Hamon, Apostle
Vision Church
Author of *7 Anointings for Kingdom Transformation*

Dr. Greg Hood has written a very necessary book for the body of Christ at this critical time. It is an apostolic foundation for us to stand upon and will give context and order to our Kingdom call. *The Gospel of the Kingdom* has been written by a scholar who loves the word of God and has communicated in a fresh and direct way exactly what the Lord was sent by the Father to do and why we are being equipped, "For such a time as this". The Kingdom assignments that are before us will require binding the strongman and plundering the enemy. Cunning strategy from the Lord along with the reality of the authority He gave us is the only way we will accomplish what He wills, "on earth as it is in heaven."

This book has laid the axe to some religious roots we have held on to in spite of there being no scriptural basis. I thank God for it. I felt we must be for our generation what John the Baptist was to his generation. John was carrying the transitional steps forward and modeling the new priesthood, not one made by a religious structure but rather, one formed by the fire of God - not watered down or distracted from his kingdom focus. John was to the Priesthood in his generation as David was in his generation in the innovative execution of the Lord's Tabernacle to bring down the revelation and God's rule. I was challenged by this book and excited at what it will release to the corporate body. This book is a call for all of us to stand up and do what we have been sent to do.

Anne S Tate
International Director of Prayer and the Watches
Glory of Zion, International

The Gospel of the Kingdom is one of the most important messages that undergirds much of our understanding of Scripture and the relationship between man and God. Jesus who was a perfect man and God incarnate made the Gospel of the Kingdom the essence of his preaching while he was on earth making the Gospel of the Kingdom the most important message Jesus ever preached and that he expects his followers all over the world to emulate. I am convinced that much of the body of Christ is weak because of a lack of understanding of the Gospel of the Kingdom. My dear friend Dr. Greg Hood's book completely changes that unfortunate trajectory by reintroducing much of the body of Christ to the Gospel of the Kingdom. I highly recommend this powerful book for anyone who is serious about personal transformation and the transformation of culture.

Dr. Francis Myles
Author: *The Order of Melchizedek*
Founder: Francis Myles International

THIS BOOK! Here it is, an astoundingly simple yet profound picture of the Kingdom of God. Greg does such a great job of bringing the truth out about God's original intention, what He had in mind to do, from "...before the foundation of the world." This book clears up all the questionable things we have heard and been taught regarding His will, His character, His heart for humanity and His Kingdom purpose. It's a MUST READ!

Apostle Randy Lopshire
Riverside Church
Clarksville, TN

My family and I have gotten to know Greg and Joan Hood, not only in a spiritual leadership way, but also in a personal way.

They are true, kind and wise ... beyond their years

This book is an amazing read. Greg's wisdom and interpretation of scripture is so insightful and energizing! Everyone needs a copy of this book as a guideline for life and salvation! We are proud to know and love this man of God and have the utmost confidence in him.

Shalom to all!
Lily Isaacs and the Isaacs Family
Members of the Grand Ole Opry
Winner of 7 Dove Awards
2-time Grammy Nominee

I have read dozens of books on the Kingdom. Most of them leave me wanting more clarity. I have preached on the Kingdom for 25 of my 36 years of ministry, and I always had a sense of wanting more revelation than I had. Dr. Greg Hood has solved my problem with his book, *The Gospel of the Kingdom*. Greg has placed a spiritual magnifying glass on the Gospels and enlarged for us the revelation of the Kingdom. His explanation of terminology and his excellent ability to show us the contrast in terms makes this book the most practical and helpful book on the Kingdom I've ever read. I'm certainly not an expert on the Bible, but I have been studying it diligently for well over half my life and I learned more about the Kingdom in Greg's book than any other I've read on the subject. Thank you, Dr. Greg Hood, for enriching our lives with this work!

Dr. Dwain Miller
President of Dwain Miller Ministries
Senior Pastor of The Edge Church Cabot, Arkansas

If there is one subject, we ought to understand to fulfill our biblical mandate with great impact. It is the Kingdom and its message. Since the Kingdom of God is all about His authority, the rulership and purpose it requires, first, announcement to welcome it, which was the core ministry of John the Baptist. Second, it demands recognition; "the kingdom that is at hand." Third, usher in with sincere prayer; "Let your kingdom come." The focus and power of hour prayer as we declare, with confidence as children, for His will be done. Fourth, it demands following wholeheartedly by making our priority; "Seek first His kingdom," which is the foundation and sources of all true blessings.

The Lord Jesus as our high priest and king started His ministry by announcing the coming of the Kingdom. During his earthly ministry, he demonstrated the power and authority of the Kingdom. After he conquered death and secured all authorities both on Earth and the heavens, he explained the reality of the Kingdom to His disciples for 40 days in preparing them for the Great Commission of discipling nations. Discipling is to bring about behavior change for lasting transformation by demonstrating the kingdom value and culture which includes life, love, peace, and power through the Holy Spirit and many characteristics. Hence, understand the Kingdom and apply kingdom principles, as we demonstrate the power of the Gospel of the Kingdom. That is why *The Gospel of the Kingdom,* by author Dr. Greg Hood, is very timely and important for the Body of Christ.

I recommend you read this book with an open mind for the renewal and transformation of your value system so that we can to at the end "I have brought you glory on earth by completing the work you gave me to do" (John 17:4).

Dr. Alemu Beeftu, Ph.D.
Gospel of Glory Ministries

There is a fresh wind of God blowing across the globe, and it is the wind of the Kingdom, and Dr. Greg Hood has captured that wind in *The Gospel of the Kingdom*. With a distinct clarity that does not get lost in manufactured theology, this book takes you behind the curtain, drawing out truths and parallels that God has designed to ignite the passion of the kingdom.

The fresh breath of God upon this work is that it does not leave you with a knowledge that is only applicable behind the pulpit; it paves a way forward for the people of God to launch the power of the kingdom that brings restoration to the *kosmos* and your world as well.

Upon your conclusion of reading this book, like me, you will be encouraged, enlightened, and empowered to step into your anointing and authority as a prophet, priest, and king, but more importantly, as a son or daughter of the King. The contents of this book will bring conformity in your life to the "laws, authority and dominion of the Creator." It is your destiny, your purpose, and any unhealthy belief structure that has been aligned against who you were created to be will be broken.

Dr. Greg Hood is a brother born for the battle, and in this classic work on the kingdom, his sword is drawn, his shield is locked with yours, and the victory is nigh!

Dr. Scott Reece, Senior Leader
River City Church
Moline, IL

Does your personal baggage effect how you experience the Word of God? Dr. Greg Hood teaches you how to unravel the filters of your life to discover the simplicity and clarity of Kingdom insight. His down home "redneck" style of breaking down the Kingdom Gospel is from his heart, and you will feel his love with every word.

Curtis Hill
Indiana's 43rd Attorney General

Greg Hood has written a masterpiece, one that readers will be mining for years. Never a person to shy from controversial positions, Greg presents the truth of the Kingdom of God as revealed through scripture. The strength of this book is its presentation of an unabashed blueprint for kingdom foundation, a gospel not just of salvation or personal fulfillment but of the assembling of all believers into the fully functional Kingdom of God. Greg blends folksy wit with profound sights, striking to the core of Jesus' ministry on earth. In so doing, he reveals our purpose, our destiny, and our fulfillment as sons and daughters of God. It is impossible to read this work without rising to our rightful places in the kingdom—following the King and embracing all of heaven throughout the earth.

Dr. Harold R. Eberle – Worldcast Ministries, author of *Father-Son Theology*, and many other books.

Raised in the church, like many of you, I grew up knowing the Gospel of Salvation but had very little if any understanding of the Gospel of the Kingdom.

Many years ago, Holy Spirit began taking me through a journey of transformation from knowing Christ through the eyes of church-life to knowing Him by the Word and Spirit. I can remember spending hours reading, studying, praying, and asking questions wanting to know "what is the Kingdom"? I knew about salvation. I loved and had a deep desire to know Jesus more and to make Him known. I loved the Word and sought to follow its commands. I knew what church was (well, not really, but I thought I did!) I had an idea of what heaven would be like (sort of). But what is this thing called the Kingdom? And what is the Gospel of the Kingdom? Is it just the Gospel of salvation, or is there more?

Oh, to have had this book back then!! What a gift that would have been to help in my searching.

Get your highlighter, pen, and paper ready, and prepare to dig into a marvelous feast of truth. Along the way, you will undoubtedly stop to ponder, probably laugh out loud and maybe even release a shout or at least a gasp as you go on a journey of discovery. Following the example of Jesus, the Master Teacher who would often say to His disciples, "You have heard it said, but I say unto you . . . ", Greg will present Kingdom truth that challenges the traditions of religion. And he does it with Biblical scholarship, grace, humor, and at times, poignant statements that will cause you to pause to take it all in.

My friend, Greg Hood, has done a powerful job presenting truth, confronting what many of us learned through tradition, religion, and doctrinal errors, in his new work, and calling us all to live more fully in *The Gospel of the Kingdom*. I highly recommend that you don't just read these pages; devour them; study them.

Jacquie Tyre, Apostle
Jacquie Tyre Ministries

This Yankee born in Iowa, but raised in Texas, wants to thank a Redneck and theologian from Mississippi in helping his readers understand the simplicity of what God's kingdom is all about. Dr. Greg Hood has done a masterful job at not only releasing truth regarding the kingdom but also releasing the methodology in understanding those truths. While being led by the Spirit of God, he helps the reader to take apart a passage in order to receive its full understanding and the truth that is ready to leap from the pages of God's word. For years I have been preaching and teaching how essential it is to move out of the religious systems of this world and all the false church structures and traditions that have held people captive. Greg has helped immensely in helping us not only understand but to be embraced by the very presence and truth of God. He brings us back to a wonderful and powerful understanding of God's original intent for His church, His Ekklesia! We will pray, and witness His kingdom and will being done on earth as it is in heaven.

Dr. Thomas Schlueter, Apostle
Texas Apostolic Prayer Network, Director
Prince of Peace House of Prayer
Arlington, Texas

I appreciate this much needed book explaining the powerful message of the kingdom. The word "kingdom" has been misused, stolen, overlooked, glossed over, or just plain ignored. Dr. Greg Hood is a powerful, revelatory writer who demonstrates through this book the ability to bring into clarity the message of bringing heaven to earth through the establishment of the rule of God through His people. Don't let Apostle Greg's simplistic style fool you. Sometimes genius disguises itself in simple language that we can all grasp. This message is right on time as we, the body of Christ, step into our true calling to make earth look like heaven.

Regina Shank
Global Transformation International

I just read the manuscript of Dr. Greg Hood's book *The Gospel of the Kingdom* that contains prophetic revelation genuinely inspired by the Spirit of God. I have been inspired by the insight and fresh interpretation of Scriptures regarding Prayer, Faith, and understanding of the Word! This book is filled with spiritual truths that will bring light to the mundane. Looking to be challenged, well look no more.

If we keep the light of God's truth shining brightly, we have a greater chance of avoiding deception. Enjoy your journey in truth and freedom, through every page!

Paulette Polo
Founder of Mantle of Power Ministries

Greg Hood's *The Gospel of the Kingdom* is an apostolic message delivered with a prophetic axe that strategically lays to the root twisted religious theology that has held the church captive for centuries. This book is a plumbline in the hand of the Lord, that is being placed over the structures of His church in this hour which is endowed with an anointing to make every crooked place straight. Direct and to the point, the revelation and teaching in this book has been penned with simplicity and a down to earth approach making it palatable and easy to digest for every believer. I love the way Greg unpacks the scriptures in Greek and Hebrew using every-day language laced with southern humor that invites any believer, young or old, to understand hidden truths of the Gospel of the Kingdom. I encourage you as you read this book to allow the structures of your theology to be measured against this plumbline of truth and see crooked places become aligned and made stable and the freedom of Christ and his kingdom burst forth in your life as a result.

Dr. Anita Alexander, Th.D.
Senior minister Golden City Church, Revival Flame Ministries, Kingdom Academy School of the Supernatural
Gold Coast, Australia
www.revival-flame.org

Dr. Greg Hood has hit the bullseye in *The Gospel of the Kingdom*! This book is both inspirational and impactful.

There is both needed revelation and practical application, which is rare in today's Church. This is a must read as the Church moves into deeper understanding of what our identity is, what our role is, and how to bring forth transformation in people's lives and in the culture. *The Gospel of the Kingdom* is a great tool for the People of God in every Nation!

Bob Long, Apostle
Rally Call Leadership Network
Rally Call Ministries
www.rallycall.net
Austin, Texas

The Gospel of the Kingdom is a book that carries an assignment to reinstate and realign the church back to long lost biblical truths that in this hour will bring forth much needed maturity. This is an urgent and timely message that is a package from A – Z imparting keys in how to live a successful overcoming Christian life geared for all believers, newly saved and for those who have been long in the pews. Laid out in easy, understandable language that is easy to engage with, Greg articulately addresses and exposes stale religious manner that much of the church have been feeding on for centuries and decades. Praise God for Dr. Greg Hood and his book! I believe without a doubt this book is a key gifted to the church in this crucial hour that will help us recognize and remove wrong shaky foundations, and empower us to rebuild strong, sure, immovable foundations essential for governing with Christ.

Dr. Sasha Alexander, D. MIN., Th.D.
Senior minister Golden City Church, Revival Flame Ministries, Kingdom Academy School of the Supernatural
Gold Coast, Australia
www.revival-flame.org

Having known Dr. Greg Hood for some 40 years, I am amazed at where the LORD has taken him and how He has used him. *The Gospel of the Kingdom* is yet another amazing milestone for this man of God. The book is filled with present day truth presented in a very understandable way. I recommend it highly to all who want to understand the Kingdom and the times we are living in.

Apostle Tommy Kelly
New Wine Fellowship
Houston, MS.

The Gospel of the Kingdom is revolutionary, riveting, revitalizing, and right on time. It is the message that Jesus proclaimed, which is seldom taught in its entirety. Dr. Greg Hood delivered this revelation with pinpoint clarity using a very personable teaching style, sprinkled with just enough humor to keep me smiling throughout the book. Using an intimate approach, it seemed as if Dr. Hood was sitting and having a conversation, with just me.

This work really opened my eyes to the Father's plan and purpose for man from the beginning. Dr. Hood reveals the strategic plan of God concerning man and his place in the Kingdom, which enables the Church to fully understand it's purpose and destiny. These truths operationally orient citizens of the Kingdom and directly provoke a tactical response, to mobilize and empower God's people to take their place in every sector of society.

The world needs to hear this message, now! I imagine the universal church taking hold of this teaching, walking in the full understanding of their true place as Kingdom citizens, permeating every sector of society, taking the Kingdom to every place they set their feet. This book makes it a real possibility, today!

Keith Long, Sergeant Major, U. S. Marine Corps (Retired)
Semper Fi!

When Jesus came, he preached and manifested the Gospel of the Kingdom, this has been watered down by modern thought and reduced to far less than it was intended to be, but that was never the purpose of God! In this book Greg Hood aptly and courageously restores true biblical truth and awakens the heart to the potential of the Kingdom of God. We are told by Jesus to pray that the Kingdom would come; after reading this book, I believe that you will be praying from a deeper knowledge and expectancy! Great book, great read, and great truth!

Dennis Goldsworthy-Davis, author
Great Grace Ministries
San Antonio, TX

Con profundas y sencillas palabras el apóstol Hood , busca que recibamos la verdad de las manifestaciones y bendiciones del Reino de Dios. El ser guiado por El Espíritu Santo para saber usar el dominio Divino del Reino de Dios a través de Sus redimidos y manifestarlo a favor de otros hacia otros, es una tremenda bendición y más allá de nuestras expectativas o creencias. Excelente libro

With profound and simple words Apostle Hood seeks that we receive the truth of the manifestations and blessings of the Kingdom of God. Being guided by the Holy Spirit to know how to use the divine domain of the Kingdom of God through His redeemed ones and manifest it in favor of others towards others, is a tremendous blessing and beyond our expectations or beliefs. Excellent book.

Pastor Jorge Carranza Palomo
Destroying Fortresses House
Costa Rica

The Gospel of the Kingdom resonates in such a clear, concise, and relatable language. Apostle Greg built a foundational text that lays the scriptural groundwork for the Kingdom of God. With the eye-opening and exciting revelation of the Word, he provides understanding of why Jesus came, and Greg explains our authority in the Kingdom. At every turn, Greg shows scriptural context, backing up the validity of his teaching. Jesus came to get the kingdom back into His people's hands! Now it's our responsibility to step up! This is a great call to action. You have a role to play—get in the game!

Craig Blow, Major, U.S. Army (Retired)
Owner, Prime Remnant, Inc.

Just finished reading *The Gospel of the Kingdom*! This book explains, in a very simple way, the difference between RELIGION and THE KINGDOM. As a business owner it really gave me insight as to God's desire for His children to succeed! In other words, it is not a bad thing to be successful in business and to thrive in the marketplace! WE ARE CHILDREN OF THE KING!! Dr. Hood, thanks so much for sharing what God has shown you!

Mike Granger, Business Owner, Dream Quest, LLC

I've known Greg Hood for around four years now and every time we talk about the kingdom he lights up and now finally he writes a book about it.

This book really does teach you about the kingdom about God, His heart and how you can use the principles throughout your business, your family and all aspects love your life.

It teaches you that we are all Kings, and we are creators and need to live and think in this realm.

This book really does break it down and make it easy to understand how the Kingdom works.

Jeremy Bell
Kingdom Entrepreneurs - Australia

This powerful book is Holy Spirit's now word for today! In *The Gospel of the Kingdom*, Apostle Greg Hood uncovers the revelation of God's Kingdom. This revelation is what we in the Ekklesia, the Body of Christ, desperately need to operate in the fullness of Jesus' power, authority, and destiny. After Jesus' death on the Cross and resurrection from the grave, He spent forty days with His apostles before He ascended into heaven. During this vital time before He left, what did Jesus do? Whatever it was, we know it was very, very important. Luke tells what Jesus did, "He spoke constantly of the kingdom of God" (Acts 1:3 Voice Bible). For forty days all Jesus talked about was the Kingdom of God: it's that important. In *The Gospel of the Kingdom* Apostle Greg reveals the importance of this truth. So, read this book, renew your mind, and release the Kingdom of God on the earth!

Lt Col (Ret.) James Mark Massa
Sons of the Branch Ministries

Teacher and author of "God's Heart of War Series" including: The War Songs of God, The War Cries of God, and The War Dances of God.

Greg's insights and understanding of the kingdom and praying heaven to earth are real eye openers that will deeply impact your spiritual walk and relationship with God.

Lars Brittsjo
Business Owner
Singapore

Over the last 40 years of walking with the Lord, I have only personally met a handful of people whom I have sensed that deep physical, tangible, weighty presence of our wonderful God, woven into all aspects of their lives. Apostle Greg is one of those few.

When he puts pen to paper, that weightiness, that presence, pours out as revelation that Holy spirit has shown him.

This book is exactly that. Holy Spirit breathed teaching and revelation for such a time as this.

The depth, magnitude and ramifications of this revelation stopped me in my tracks many times as I began reading the manuscript. I could not simply read through it and enjoy it as a "good read" or view it as "great revelation", but had to continually stop, prayerfully process its content, allow it to penetrate my understanding and world view, and challenge my theology. I view this book as one that I want to read several times over the next few years to allow it to fully sink in.

I genuinely believe that this book is essentially a "Kingdom Manual" for believers, and it contains the seeds of a grassroots, world-wide Kingdom Movement that believers can sow their lives into.

Thank you, mate, for your time, effort, and obedience to Holy Spirit in writing this book.

Kevin Philippa, Business Owner,
Platinum Care Services
Queensland Australia

The Gospel of
the Kingdom

Greg Hood

Copyright

The Gospel of the Kingdom

by Greg Hood

Word studies in the Greek and Hebrew are taken from:

- Strong's Concordance
- Brown-Driver-Briggs Hebrew and English Lexicon
- AMG's Annotated Dictionary of the Old and New Testament ©1984, 1990, 2008
- The Complete Word Study Dictionary: Old Testament by Warren Baker and Eugene Carpenter ©2003
- The Complete Word Study Dictionary: New Testament compiled by Spiros Zodhiates ©1992

Edit/Layout by Jim Bryson (JamesLBryson@gmail.com)

Cover design by David Munoz (davidmunoznvtn@gmail.com)

Contact Info

Dr. Greg Hood
Greg Hood Ministries
PO Box 22, Amory, MS 38821
office@greghood.org

Dedication

I DEDICATE THIS BOOK to two men who greatly influenced my life, men whom I love with all my heart.

First, my father, Hershel Dean Hood. He was my hero, the one whom I always wanted to be when I grew up. He was a military man, a railroad man and a hall-of-fame musician. A man's man! I remember telling him, "Daddy, if I can become half the man you are, I will consider myself a success."

That is still my sentiment today. I sure do miss him!

Second, my Father-in-Law, Wilfredo Marzo Sobrepena. He was my friend, a great role model and a boundless encouragement to me. He gave me the greatest gift anyone has ever given me—in marriage some 25 years ago: his daughter Joan. He was a teacher of teachers, a man of integrity and a steward of his family like no one I have ever encountered. Dad, I am honored to have been your pastor for over 20 years. Your wisdom and insight actually pastored me through those years.

Both of these men stepped into the Cloud of Witnesses on May 16, 2021, seven hours apart from one another, on two different continents.

I love you both, and I dedicate this work to you.

Acknowledgments

I WANT TO THANK MY WIFE, Joan, who has been with me on this wonderful and challenging journey of having our school of thought reshaped, from that of a strong religious mindset to a kingdom mindset. She has been a rock of support and endured my teachings and sermons on this topic hundreds of times. We have come a long way, and I know the journey is not yet over. This book has been burning in my heart for some time now. There is no way it could have come about without her help and guidance through this whole process. Thank you, Sinta Ko ("My Love")!

A very special thanks to my editor, Jim Bryson. You are not only a great editor, but you have become a wonderful friend. I am thankful. Working through this manuscript has been an enjoyable journey.

To everyone who wrote a foreword, an endorsement or gave me theological insight (and correction, from time to time), I am eternally grateful. You have impacted my life in very special ways. I am thankful for our friendships.

A special thank you to Pastor Terry Garrett and Carrol McDonnell, for assisting in proofreading.

Last but certainly not least, I want to thank the friends, mentors and fathers in the faith who, throughout my ministry, have challenged me to embrace a theology that was more kingdom minded and not religious. Men like Dr. Raymond Biard, Dr. Joseph Thornton, Pastor Cecil Pumphrey and Carrol Pettigrew, to name a few.

Faithful are the wounds of a friend

Proverbs 27:6

A friend loves at all times,
And a brother is born for adversity.

Proverbs 17:17

Contents

1ˢᵗ Foreword

By Dutch Sheets

I GREW UP UNDER THE ERRONEOUS BELIEF that the Kingdom of God would not exist until sometime in the future, with a 1000-year reign of Christ on the earth. We simply called it "the Millennial Reign." This was accompanied by a belief that things would get worse on earth, including in the Church, until Jesus rescued us through the rapture. We believers would then be in heaven for seven years, after which we would return to earth with Him for this 1000-year reign.

Because of this mindset, seeking first the Kingdom of God meant living in such a way as to one day be part of something off in the distant future. Praying "Thy Kingdom come, thy will be done" was asking for the rapture and this millennial reign to take place. Preaching the gospel of the Kingdom was preaching a message intended to prepare people for heaven, not to impact the earth.

Since our theology meant that conditions on earth must get worse and worse before Christ could return, there was no reason to work for societal change (and we didn't!). Nor was there any reason to strive for the Church to become stronger and more effective. To have preached that those things could occur would have been heretical to us and, besides, they would delay Christ's return. Therefore, we were trapped in a conundrum: we did not like to see evil increase and the effectiveness of the Church decrease, yet we were also told to rejoice because that meant our redemption was drawing near. Talk about spiritual schizophrenia!

In 1977, I enrolled in Christ For the Nations Institute, in Dallas, Texas. Jim Hodges was part of the faculty, and I soon became convinced he was one of the greatest teachers I had ever heard. Professor Hodges taught a course entitled "The Kingdom of God." I was expecting a class on eschatology (which I wasn't excited about). What I experienced was a course on the rule and authority of Christ—yesterday, today, and forever. My head spun, my heart came alive, and my world changed forever. Theology became exciting, the earth became changeable, and reigning with Christ became NOW! A King in waiting was now a King in action. And my desire to be raptured was replaced by a desire to occupy until He comes. My faith became active! The "leaven of the Kingdom" had worked its way into my religious mind, conforming it more accurately to the mind of Christ.

Greg Hood's book, *The Gospel of the Kingdom*, will have the same impact on you. It will bring hope for the present, as well as for eternity. A dominion mindset will replace an escapism mindset. You will find yourself excited about ruling and reigning with Christ here on earth, in the here and now. Confusing passages of Scripture will finally make sense, and murky theological concepts will become clear.

Read this enlightening book with an open mind and heart. Ask Holy Spirit to bring revelation to you through Greg's words. Ask God to free You from any wrong teaching and misguided theology holding you back from becoming everything Christ intends you to be.

You are starting an important journey. Fasten your seatbelt and enjoy the ride!

Dr. Dutch Sheets—Internationally recognized author, teacher and speaker.

2nd Foreword

By Chuck Pierce

ONE OF THE CLASSIC CHRISTMAS STORIES that is watched during the holiday season is It's a Wonderful Life. This 1946 Christmas fantasy, directed by Frank Capra, is based on a short story and booklet by Phillip Van Doren Stern called The Greatest Gift. This story is about George Bailey, a smalltown individual with a longing to travel worldwide. However, the burdens and responsibilities of family and friends destine him to never leave Bedford Falls, New York. The Bailey brothers owned and operated the Building and Loan which helps "the little people" of the town. After the death of his father, George inherits the burden of this family business. Their biggest adversary is Henry F. Potter, who controls most of the town, including the bank.

On each eve of his long-awaited escape, when George first plans a world tour before college and then for his honeymoon, crises arise. Mr. Potter does everything he can to shut down the Building and Loan to obtain ultimate control of the entire colonized region. George finally succumbs to the pressure and burdens of trying to keep the city free from the control of his adversary. But, through the prayers of his friends and family, God sends angelic help through an angel named Clarence. As the angel confronts George, who has just wished he had never been born, the angel grants him his wish. The following scenes of the movie are about what life would be without a "kingdom minded person" involved in the city. This picture is an incredible display of understanding the Kingdom of Heaven, God's rule, and the Kingdom of God within us. If the Lord has no one for the Kingdom of Heaven to rule in the earth realm, darkness will overtake that portion of the earth.

The Gospel of the Kingdom, by Greg Hood, is one of the most important books for today. In my ministry and life, I've had approximately 40 books published. Each book in some way reflects Kingdom life on earth as we serve as ambassadors of the Kingdom of

Heaven. The Kingdom of God is within us. When God knit us together in our mother's womb, He knit the capacity for the Kingdom of Heaven to enter and dwell with man. Through the sacrifice of His son shedding His blood and redeeming mankind, mankind has the capacity for Yeshua to rule through us. Because God is Father of our spirits, He knit our spirit man with the ability to have and enjoy life in abundance. However, we must choose to rule in a fallen world that has already been redeemed. How we submit our spirit-man to the life of God through the blood of His Son and by His Spirit is the main focus of us demonstrating the Kingdom here on earth.

When Yeshua died, He descended and liberated hell, and then ascended and gave gifts to mankind. He thoroughly defeated His adversary, the "father of lies," Satan. If Satan would have known what the Cross would accomplish, he would have never used that as his mode to try to defeat God's redeeming plan. The victory of the Cross and the power of the resurrection completely defeated Satan's desire to rule the earth. However, each person must choose to enforce that rule in their sphere of authority. Without mankind choosing and exercising the authority of heaven here on earth, Satan attempts to continue his rule.

I can still remember when God showed me all of the blessings that were meant for me in heaven. I was a young executive for the oil industry in Houston. I would spend my quiet time with God when carpooling or riding the bus to work. One day on the way home, I was reading Ephesians 1:3, when the quickening power of the Spirit of God within me came alive as I read these words: "Blessed and worthy of praise be the God and Father of our Lord Jesus Christ, who has blessed us with every spiritual blessing in the heavenly realms in Christ, just as [in His love] He chose us in Christ [actually selected us for Himself as His own] ..." (AMP). I came to realize that the acts people do in the earth cannot be compared to how God created the blessings for each one of us, before the foundation of the world.

All of the sudden, such a dynamic of ascension occurred in my life, as faith filled me beyond any way I had been filled before. I had so much faith in me on that bus that I was akin to Paul – not knowing if I was on the bus (on the earth) or in heaven. God showed me the blessings that He had for my entire bloodline. He then said, "Your dad, your grandfather and other members of your family never chose these blessings. If you choose, you can have all of these Kingdom blessings that I intended through the ages for your bloodline." Suddenly, I saw Kingdom rule that had been squandered at times in family members. I made a choice to operate in Kingdom authority so that I could not only restore things that had been lost but also access the many blessings that had never been gained. The Kingdom of Heaven became real to me. However, I knew that the only way the Kingdom of Heaven could be manifested on earth in my life was to demonstrate in the earth realm what I saw in Heaven. Kingdom rule became a reality! My body was pulsating with faith from seeing the Kingdom of Heaven. I asked the Lord to show me what to do with the faith in me and He said, "Give it away." Each time we worship the Lord, we ascend by His Spirit and gain access to the blessings we have in the Kingdom of Heaven. We then descend and go to war to enforce those blessings in the earth.

I have read few books that explain Kingdom rule for the Body of Christ as well as *The Gospel of the Kingdom*. Greg Hood has created a masterpiece. We truly do have a "wonderful life" when we exercise life as God intended for us to display during our time here on the earth. "Who you are" is how you demonstrate God's Kingdom purpose in the world, in your sphere of authority.

Dr. Chuck D. Pierce—President of Glory of Zion International, Kingdom Harvest Alliance, and Global Spheres Inc.

Introduction

WHEN I WAS A BOY GROWING UP in the deep south, I traveled with my grandfather to various churches within our denomination. He preached a simple message: the gospel of salvation. By that, he meant salvation—that we are all sinners, but if we accept God's grace, Jesus would save us and we would go to heaven. And if we didn't accept Jesus? "Well boy, if you think Mississippi's hot…"

The gospel of salvation. It got a lot of people through the door of churches, but…it didn't get them any further. Live a good religious life, support the local church, keep things between the navigational buoys, and an angel band will be waiting to take you to heaven when you die.

Later in life, I pondered on all I saw in my formative years—the church pews filled with good people, some religious zealots haranguing the flock, and a few outright hypocrites masquerading as sheep. Most church people were trying in earnest to measure up to the standards set before them. I knew God loved them and they loved God, but something was missing. Churches came and went. Preachers came and went. Revivals lifted congregations like a tide, but then the tide went out. Where was the victorious church Jesus spoke of?

Then I saw it.

While this gospel of salvation pulled from certain scriptures, it missed many more. In fact, it missed the key scriptures of Jesus' message. I realized that Jesus did not come merely to get people "saved." His message was not: "Pray this prayer or go to hell." Rather, Jesus' message was embodied in the prayer he taught his disciples in Matthew 6: "Your kingdom come. Your will be done on earth as it is in heaven."

Looking further, Jesus' intentions were clear: "I will build my ekklesia (Church), my government." (ref. Matthew 16:18)

Suddenly, the focus on individual salvation, with the much-touted "personal relationship with the Lord Jesus Christ," seemed incomplete.

Yes, it was great that people were getting saved. Yet it was a celebration of new birth without any thought to the child's future—her schooling, her college fund, her contributions to society. We were minting fledgling Christians and saying, "You've escaped the flames. Have a seat. You're along for the ride. Next stop, heaven!"

All of this, at the expense of what Jesus actually came to do. "The Son of God appeared for this purpose, to destroy the works of the devil" (1 John 3:8). The works of the devil are much more than the purported eternal suffering of hell. And destroying them means more than "getting people saved." Jesus came to establish a kingdom.

The Kingdom of God is made of people fulfilling what Adam failed to fulfill. Each of us is a part of the whole. Certainly, God could wipe the earth clean and start over, but instead, he's given that task to us. And indeed, the drive is in us. It's in our desires, our anguish, our hopes, our deeds, our prayers, our declarations, our resolve. Like uranium ore deep in rock, we radiate all that the Father has set within us and before us.

The calling of the Father is not just to personal salvation. The cause is too large to accomplish alone. The saint who prays for a new car may receive God's answer, but it's the car company that builds it—a company united in purpose, led with integrity, and committed to outcome.

Likewise, we—the redeemed of God—are seeking in earnest all that we have been promised and even that which we cannot conceive of as yet. It will come, but not through individual effort. It will come through kingdom, one comprised of each of us. A thousand rifle bearers do not make an army, but an army is comprised of a thousand rifle bearers. It is not up to each of us but to all of us...united under the King.

The Kingdom of God is among us, but we must assemble as a kingdom. In these pages, I will show you how and why.

1

The Gospel of the Kingdom

EVERYTHING WE LEARN IN LIFE IS FILTERED THROUGH OURSELVES—all that we have learned through experience and study, and all that we are through our personalities, talents and perspectives. This is not necessarily a bad thing until we discover that some of our filtering is giving us the wrong answers.

In this book, I am offering the means to shift your religion as it has never shifted before. The impact will be far-reaching and lasting. Our lives will shift. Our families will shift. Our ministries will shift. Our communities, states and nations will shift.

What I will be teaching is by no means my ideas alone. Indeed, it comes from Holy Spirit. Because of the unique nature of the subject, some of this might take some processing alone with God until you are comfortable with it. That's to be expected. I'm presenting concepts that have taken God years to impress upon me. Yet it is all Holy Spirit-inspired.

Now, I do have a doctorate degree in theology, and many people say, "Wow, that is pretty awesome!" The truth is, it's worthless. Most of what I learned in seminary was not what I needed to walk with God. Without Holy Spirit, it is easy to be miseducated. Certainly, there was some worth to the education process. I learned the discipline of study. However, the subjects I studied were more geared toward promoting a religious perspective than kingdom insight. So, while it is entirely possible for me to create my own theological positions, I have learned to rely on Holy Spirit for my insight, direction and content. I have learned to live the truth of Jesus' words to his disciples in the hours before he left the earth:

> *But the Helper, the Holy Spirit whom the Father will send in*
> *My name, He will teach you all things, and remind you of all*
> *that I said to you.*
>
> John 14:26

In learning anything new, especially something monumental, there is required a letting go of what we have believed to make way for what is replacing it. This is a conscious act of our will. We cannot love our old beliefs to the extent that we hang on to them more than revealed truth. Paul understood this as the principle behind Christian growth.

> *Not that I have already grasped it all or have already become*
> *perfect, but I press on if I may also take hold of that for which*
> *I was even taken hold of by Christ Jesus. Brothers and sisters,*
> *I do not regard myself as having taken hold of it yet; but one*
> *thing I do: forgetting what lies behind and reaching forward*
> *to what lies ahead, I press on toward the goal for the prize of*
> *the upward call of God in Christ Jesus.*
>
> Philippians 3:12-14

Jesus said it even more succinctly.

You will know the truth and the truth will make you free.

> John 8:32 (NLV)

How will we know what is truth?

It will make us free.

How do we know that we need this truth?

We are not free.

Good teaching will show us where we are not free, and then it will free us. It is with that goal in mind that we embark on this present field of study.

Now, for those who don't know me, I am from the deep south of the United States. I am a redneck. (And proud of it!) As such, I tend to make things simple. I believe that if you can't explain your theology to a 5-year-old, you might have to rethink it. God's truth is not complicated. Consequently, our study will not be like a traditional school of thought. This will be: "Let us walk through this thing simply." Amen!

At the outset, I said that we all filter information. This is normal. In fact, it is necessary. Without filtering—some folks call it interpretation—nothing we experience can make any sense. Interpretation means that we assign value to what we see and hear. It's how we process information.

For example, if I say "cat," every reader will assign a value to the arrangement of those three letters C-A-T. Some will see a furry creature that likes to sit on your lap and be petted...or not...depending on its disposition. Some older folks who actually remember the 60s might see a good jazz musician, as in "That cat has a cool downbeat." Still others, perhaps with construction experience, will see a 60-ton bulldozer—a D-9 Caterpillar commonly called a "Cat." Not something you want sitting on your lap.

So, we have to ask ourselves some questions to help us understand how we are interpreting what we read in the Word of God.

1. WHO IS SPEAKING?

When we study the Word of God, we need to understand the perspective of the writer and, more importantly, the perspective of the speaker being recorded.

Now, I am not talking about God; he is always talking. Holy Spirit breaths the Word of God. We understand that. But in studying scripture, we must ask: Was Holy Spirit speaking when the passage was recorded? Just because something is in the Bible does not make it truth. Sometimes the Bible records barbaric or despicable acts to make a point. The Bible is unflinchingly honest. That does not mean we follow every example we find there. For example, David committed adultery with Bathsheba and murdered her husband to cover up the resultant pregnancy. Is that an example we are to follow? Of course not. Certainly, God had a reason for recording this, but it was clearly not for us to follow. We are to filter; we are to interpret; we are to think; we are to seek Holy Spirit for understanding. Let us be wise, mature and open to God's wonderful Spirit who teaches us all things. Let us have simple hearts and ready ears to receive it.

2. WHO ARE THEY SPEAKING TO?

Asking who the speakers were talking to enables us to discern the culture for which the message or word was being applied. There are idioms that were used in those cultures that don't make sense today. In fact, they mean something totally different to us in modern culture.

We see this everywhere. Expressions in America don't make sense in England. Even expressions in Indiana don't make sense in Mississippi (where I am from). It took me a while to learn this, but as I traveled the United States and the world, speaking my native tongue, I often got asked: "What do you mean?"

I might say to a friend from New York: "We're fixin' to carry Momma to the Piggy Wiggly."

And he'd reply: "What's a Piggly Wiggly? Why are you carrying your mother? And why are you fixing anything? Is it broke?"

Now apply that to a document recorded thousands of years ago and spanning vast cultures, with a lot more at stake than getting Mom stocked up with grits and biscuits, and you'll see why Jesus promised us Holy Spirit as a teacher before he left the earth. We need him!

3. WHAT DOES IT MEAN IN THAT CULTURE?

We must ask ourselves: What did these words and/or actions mean to the people involved? See, we never learned this in Bible college or seminary. Instead, we were given the interpretation that best fit the perspective of the religious organization supporting the school. The fact is, most of the things we get from the Word of God are filtered through our Western culture—one that is foreign to the writers of the Bible.

Why is this important? Because we read through our ideology, then develop a philosophy, which eventually forms a belief system—some folks call this a worldview. This is why God must deal with our B.S. (it stands for Belief System) before he can lead us into greater truth. Remember Jesus' words:

> *"No one sews a patch of unshrunk cloth on an old garment; otherwise, the patch pulls away from it, the new from the old, and a worse tear results. And no one puts new wine into old wineskins; otherwise the wine will burst the skins, and the wine is lost and the skins as well; but one puts new wine into fresh wineskins."*

Mark 2:21-22

God will deal with our old wineskins, but only if we allow him to. This is not always pleasant. Yet we must constantly challenge our present reality, working with Holy Spirit to ask ourselves:

- Where are we?
- What are we doing?
- Why are we doing it?

In so doing, we allow ourselves to draw closer to the truth. In so doing, we'll find a lot that we have to unlearn. Jesus told us that God's Word is truth. So then, out of our godly philosophy, we can develop a theology—how we relate to God.

4. HOW DO WE APPLY THIS?

The final act in processing truth is to apply it to our lives. But how? How do we bring new knowledge and experience to our lives and the lives of those we influence? How does the seed of truth grow?

When we bring truth into our lives, we cannot alter it. We cannot change it. We cannot say, "This is how it fits where I live." The gospel of the kingdom is not fluid; it is set in stone. This is God's idea of who he is. And I think he has a pretty good idea of who he is. In fact, his idea is pretty cool.

So, as we study the Word, we are going to ask:

- Who said it?
- Who was it said to?
- What did it mean to them?
- How do we bring it into our lives?

This simple pattern applied to the study of the Bible will bring freedom and revelation to us. Therefore, let us seek to remove, bind and destroy the Western cultural filter we have allowed to filter the Word of God. We must come against our traditions that have made the Word of God ineffective, and learn to embrace the complete truth of all God has revealed to mankind.

PRAY THIS WAY

There is a reason God's Word is not working in our families, communities and nations. It is because God is not obligated to make his Word work according to our application. It has to be according to his intent. That is why Jesus said:

Pray, then, this way:

> *Our Father, who is in heaven,*
> *Hallowed be Your name.*
> *Your kingdom come.*
> *Your will be done,*
> *On earth as it is in heaven.*

Matthew 6:9-10

Indeed, here is our first application of the four steps of inquiry. Do you realize that *prayer* in this passage is not a religious term? It is a legal term. Remember our steps:

- Who said it?
- Who was it said to?
- What did it mean to them?
- How do we bring it into our lives?

The term *prayer* is used in a legal setting. It is a governmental word. Therefore, Jesus' words in Mathew 6 can be understood as: "When you pray, you are doing government business with the Father."

GOD OF HEAVEN

It is telling that when Jesus refers to his Father, he also gives the Father's geographical location. The phrase: "Our Father who is in heaven" sets up the next phrase: "Your kingdom come. Your will be done." Where does this happen? "On earth." How does it happen? By applying: "On earth as it is in heaven."

So, in this prayer, Jesus is saying that when we pray, we should not be praying, "My will be done," but "the Father's will be done." The word *prayer* here in the Greek is *proseuchomai,* derived from the Greek word *pros* which means "motion towards a place; or to invoke or arouse one's will towards a place." Then, literally, it means "the intent of God's heart *in motion towards earth*." When we pray, we are not praying prayers from the intent of our hearts, as in "Well, Father, this is my heart for this thing." No, that is an illegal prayer. We are to pray from God's heart.

Of course, we all know that God gives us the desires of our hearts, as we are told in Psalm 37:4. But to understand this passage, we must differentiate between *intent* and *desire*. Look closer at the scripture.

> *Delight yourself in the L*ORD*;*
> *And He will give you the desires of your heart.*

Notice the order of progression here. What comes first? "Delight yourself in the Lord." What comes next? "He will give you...." When your desires become God's desires, he will give you the desires of your heart. See, in a kingdom, your opinion matters little. Only the opinion of the king matters. In the Kingdom of God, nobody's opinion matters but God's.

Now, the king may ask for counsel, but that is different. God may ask his people for counsel, but he is doing so to allow us to contribute as a minority stakeholder. We are part of the council of the Lord. From the perspective of a kingdom and the intent of the Father's heart, however, it is the purpose of the Father's heart that makes all the difference. That's all that matters. So, let us shift our thinking. We are not operating in our own purpose or calling. Everything we do must be about the Kingdom of God—the place where God is king.

Jesus expressed this to his parents at an early age (though I suspect he was born knowing it).

> *And He [Jesus] said to them, "Why did you seek Me? Did you not know that I must be about My Father's business?"*

Luke 2:49 NKJV

Jesus knew who he worked for, even though he was the Son. He never came to the earth to give us a religion. Nothing Jesus did was religious. In fact, every time he encountered religious people, he got in trouble. He said this to his mother when he was 12 years old, astounding those that were in the temple. But for every other time Jesus entered the Temple or engaged religious people, he railed against their system of observances and their corruption of all that was holy. He even got violent, turning over the heavy stone tables of the money changers and driving them from the temple with a whip.

No, Jesus never came to give us religion in any capacity. In fact, he was anathema to religion.

THE PURPOSE OF JESUS

Here is what scripture says about the purpose of Jesus.

> *The one who practices sin is of the devil; for the devil has been sinning from the beginning. The Son of God appeared for this purpose, to destroy the works of the devil.*

1 John 3:8

Look closely and apply our inquiry.

Who is speaking? *The Apostle John.*

Who is he speaking to? *The church.*

Let's discover what these words meant in their culture. Now, one of the simplest ways you can study the Word of God is with Strong's Concordance. Unlike a simple dictionary which only gives modern definitions, Strong's shows us how to trace words and find their root. This yields a word's deeper meaning.

So, where John says: "The one who practices ...." John is saying that the one who practices sin is of *the devil.* Pretty strong words.

Now: Who is speaking? Who is he talking to? What did he mean in their culture? And how am I to apply it?

When John says "the one who practices sin," is the word *sin,* plural or singular? Singular. That is important to note.

Now this phrase "is of the devil," literally does not mean that you are a devil, right? It means that you are following the devil, that you are under submission to the devil.

On the earth today, there are two kingdoms—the kingdom of darkness and the kingdom of light.

So, keeping this simple enough for a redneck to understand, when we see sin as singular, it does not mean a bunch of sins. Rather, it means one sin. John is not talking about drinking, smoking, chewing, or dating girls who do. He is not talking about the plethora of sins that constitute the actions of a sin-infested society. This term is singular, as in *one* sin.

Now, for the purpose of Jesus: "The Son of God appeared for this purpose, to destroy the works of the devil." This word *purpose* is the word *touto* in the Greek. It literally means "for this cause, assignment." It means "purpose—the same thereof, something that was in the mind of someone else." So, Jesus appeared in the earth because of something that was in someone else's mind. Whose mind do you think that was? The Father's mind.

The Father had something in his mind that caused the manifestation of Jesus upon the earth, something more than sacrifices and offerings, just as David foretold in Psalm 40:6-8.

You have not desired sacrifice and meal offering;
You have opened my ears;
You have not required burnt offering and sin offering.
Then I said, "Behold, I have come;
It is written of me in the scroll of the book.
I delight to do Your will, my God;
Your Law is within my heart."

This passage refers to Christ. It alludes to his purpose, the one that was in his Father's mind.

Back to the scripture from 1 John, we know that "the one who practices sin" (singular) is submitting to the devil, "for the devil has sinned from the beginning." This word *beginning* is the Hebrew word *arche*. It literally means "from the origin." Consider the words *beginning* and *origin*. Now, where does your mind take you? The Garden of Eden.

The root of this word *arche* is *archo*. It literally means "the beginning of rule." The beginning of rule is the beginning of dominion. *Rule* is the Hebrew word *radah* which means "dominion, the first practice of dominion." Amazing!

Growing up in a traditional, denominational Church, we were taught that these works of the devil were everything that he was trying to do in our lives. No offense to this group, but they taught me schizophrenic Christianity. They taught that once you are saved, you are always saved. They also taught that when you laid down to sleep, you should pray to God to forgive all your sins, because if you died in your sins as you slept, you were going to hell.

I struggled with this for years: "Which one is it? Am I saved? Or am I one sin away from hell?"

So, with this understanding, the Bible is saying that from the beginning, from the time that dominion (rule/*radah*) was established, the devil sinned. That takes us all the way back to the garden. Scripture is telling us that because the devil sinned from the beginning, the Son of Man (Jesus) was manifested for the purpose of destroying "the works of the devil."

Now, look at the word *appeared* in the phrase: "The Son of God appeared for this purpose." We know that Jesus has always existed. John says:

In the beginning was the Word, and the Word was with God, and the Word was God. He was in the beginning with God.

John 1:1-2

In the origin, Jesus was the Word and the Word was God. Then this happened:

And the Word became flesh, and dwelt among us;

John 1:14

We know that Jesus always was. We also know that when God created the heavens and the earth, the Father was the thinker, the creator. He spoke the Word and the Spirit covered and created it all. So, Jesus was not a new idea in the mind of the Father. Indeed, the Father and the Son are one. They have always been together as one.

This word *appeared* in the Greek is the word *phaneroo* which means "to make visible." Jesus, who always was, existed in the unseen realm in perfect time. Then, when God determined in his heart, he made Jesus visible. Jesus stepped out of the invisible realm and into the visible realm in the form of a legal agent in earth.

God designed a body for Jesus to operate on the earth. He had to. When we die, our spirit leaves; it cannot remain on earth. Why? Because it needs a body to operate legally on the earth. We are body, soul and spirit. God created us in his image, in the likeness of God.

Now, when scripture says that Jesus appeared, this word *appeared* does not just mean to make something visible, but "to make it clear in the assignment, to make a light,"

God is light. Jesus said:

"I am the Light of the world; the one who follows Me will not walk in the darkness, but will have the Light of life."

John 8:12

When Jesus appeared, he stepped out of the invisible and into the visible as light. He was the manifestation of the intent of the Father's heart. Jesus came on assignment. He did not come to get us into heaven. That was not his purpose. Nowhere does Jesus say: "My purpose is to get all y'all into heaven." Nowhere. Rather, he told us to pray:

> *Your kingdom come.*
> *Your will be done,*
> *On earth as it is in heaven.*

> Matthew 6:10

Our purpose in praying is to bring heaven to earth.

See the difference? We are not leaving earth for heaven. Heaven is coming to earth.

Certainly, when we die, if one is born-again, we go to be with God. And if we go to be with God, we will return with him when he comes back to the earth. However, God's purpose for us was never to return to heaven for eternity. Neither will we be angels when we die. When people say, "God needed another angel so he took so-and-so," it is from their hearts, which are usually hurting, but the statement is not scriptural.

Jesus was the forerunner of heaven's invasion of earth. As John says, he was on assignment for this purpose: to destroy the works of the devil. This word *destroy* is the word *luo* in the Greek. Now, *destroy* in our culture could mean something physical, like taking a hammer to a wall and beating the hell out of it. But in John, this is not what it means.

The word *destroy* is a legal term. It means "to dissolve a contract, to loose from something that is binding." It is to release one from something that is binding. In Jesus' case, it was the binding contract that Adam, a man, made with the enemy.

John's words mean "to lose from something binding, to dissolve a contract, to break one free." It refers to your year of Jubilee. You have been enslaved, you have lost your land, you have lost your influence, you have lost your voice, you do not believe. When Jubilee comes and you are freed, everything is restored back to you. When things are restored back to your family, then you are able to take those things that were restored to you and to use them for their intended purpose.

Hallelujah! This puts an end to the works of the devil.

Jesus came to earth to deal with sin. This word *sin* in the Greek is *hamartano* which means *rebellion*. It literally means "to rebel, like insurrection, to violate God's law."

When Jesus came into the world, He stepped out of the unseen realm and into the seen realm as light, with the intent of God's heart to nullify the contract made by Adam and loose humanity from the devil.

Where was this contract made? At the beginning; at the origin of dominion.

Jesus came to "destroy the works of the devil." Now this word *works* is the word *ergon* in the Greek. It does not mean the many things associated with the common concept of sin. It means "process, labor, effectual doing," as in a continuation of that rebellion. It means the effectual working that the enemy did that caused time to pass and that work to continue.

Let's look at Jesus' words from the gospel of Luke:

But He said to them, "I must also preach the kingdom of God to the other cities, because I was sent for this purpose."

Luke 4:43

There it is again. He was sent for the purpose of the Kingdom of God—that kingdom where God is King. Remember the word *purpose* means "something that someone had in their heart." Jesus came to fulfill what was in the heart of the Father. Jesus amplifies this in John 5:19:

"Truly, truly, I say to you, the Son can do nothing of Himself, unless it is something He sees the Father doing; for whatever

the Father does, these things the Son also does in the same way.

Jesus is our example. He was sent by the Father to fulfill the Father's desires. Jesus did not do anything on the earth as God. Everything he did was as a man—a sinless man—despite the fact that he had an opportunity to become sinful many times. Hebrews says:

For we do not have a high priest who cannot sympathize with our weaknesses, but One who has been tempted in all things just as we are, yet without sin.

Hebrews 4:15

Jesus understood that his God-given purpose was to preach the gospel of the Kingdom of God. It was his assignment from the heart of God. The word *gospel* means "good news." The word *kingdom* is made up of two words. It is the words *king* and *dominion*. So, when we talk about the word *king*, it means "sovereign one, majesty, the one of glory."

Who is the King of glory?
The Lord strong and mighty,
The Lord mighty in battle.

Psalm 24:8

The second part of this word is *dom*, which is the word "dominion." So, when we talk about the kingdom, we are talking about the dominion of God. Here is a definition of *dominion*.

It is the power to rule, govern, and exercise sovereignty or sovereign authority as royalty. Let me say that again. Dominion is the power to rule, govern, and exercise sovereign authority as royalty.

Any war, rebellion or struggle is a battle of opposing powers for the purpose of dominion. Man was created for dominion on earth, operating under God's delegated authority as conveyed through God's great commission. The devil deceived man and dominion passed from the hapless man to the devil. Jesus won it back for man. We are learning how to retake possession, to possess first and foremost all that Jesus won for mankind.

Let's learn all that this entails.

2

Fact From Fiction

WHEN APPLYING OUR METHODICAL INQUIRY, we will discover many cherished notions about the Kingdom of God that are just not so. The first place we see the concept of *kingdom* is in Genesis.

> Then God said, "Let Us make mankind in Our image, according to Our likeness; and let them rule over the fish of the sea and over the birds of the sky and over the livestock and over all the earth, and over every crawling thing that crawls on the earth." So God created man in His own image, in the image of God He created him; male and female He created them. God blessed them; and God said to them, "Be fruitful and multiply, and fill the earth, and subdue it; and rule over the fish of the sea and over the birds of the sky and over every living thing that moves on the earth." Then God said, "Behold, I have given you every plant yielding seed that is on the surface of all the earth, and every tree which has fruit yielding seed; it shall be food for you; and to every animal of the earth and to every bird of the sky and to everything that moves on the earth which has life, I have given every green plant for food"; and it was so. And God saw all that He had made, and behold, it was very good. And there was evening and there was morning, the sixth day.
>
> Genesis 1:26-31

First of all, when God says *man*, he is not talking about the male sex. The term *man* refers to all of us—the race of mankind. And incidentally, man only comes in two models: male and female. Gender is not like an old car that we can customize. Despite what some folks say or do, the human race is still binary: male or female. So, think *mankind* when you read *man*.

Let's look at key portions of this passage.

"Let us make man in our image, according to our likeness. And let them rule..."

Rule is from the Hebrew word *radah*. The better word is *kingdom*, meaning "to govern." So, God did not give Adam a religion. He gave Adam a kingdom—*the* kingdom.

In the garden, there were no sacrifices. There were no worship services. No pastors. No worship bands. No smoke machines. No pulpits. No skinny jeans. God did not say: "Let Adam have church." He said: "Let Adam <u>rule</u>." *Radah.*

So, when God says: "Let them rule," we could read it as: "Let them *radah*."

Recalling our method of inquiry, we might ask who God is referring to. Who is "them?" Well, if I was talking about a group of people, saying: "They went down to the store. I did not go with *them*."

Notice that when I use the word *them*, I remove myself from the group and their activities. I am not a part of *them*. It is the same when God said: "Let them *radah*." God was not ruling. "They" were ruling. Them.

To fully understand this, we have to establish something about God's relationship with man. Despite what many in the body of Christ might tell you, God is not in control of everything. We need to stop saying "God is in control." Yes, it's a pithy platitude that gives us warm fuzzies when things look grim, but it's not true. God is not in control. He is in charge, but he is not in control. In time, he will come back and take control. But for now, he removed himself from the *radah* on the Earth.

Consider these scriptures.

> The heavens are the heavens of the LORD,
> But the earth He has given to the sons of mankind.
>
> Psalm 115:16

The earth is the LORD's and the fullness thereof.

Psalm 24:1 KJV

So, the Lord owns the earth, but he put mankind in control of the earth. We understand this from the word *Lord*, which is the word *Adonai* in the Hebrew. It means "owner." So, God is the owner of the earth. When he created man, he was saying: "Let them *kingdom* the earth. Let them have *dominion* in the earth. Let them *rule* in the earth."

God is not in control; God is in charge. If God was in control, we'd have to blame him for every abortion, every murder, every divorce, every baby dying and every wife who beats her husband.

God is not in control, but this is what people are implying when they blame God for the bad things that happen. Well, if bad things are not God's fault, whose fault is it? The fact is, he put us in control— mankind, people, Adam and Company. Specifically, he put his Ekklesia in control—his church is his governmental structure in the earth.

This can be difficult for many Christians to accept. Truth like this has a wrecking ball effect on Western theology. Many folks are simply hanging out until Jesus returns. Their prayers sound like: "God, help us make it through the day. Help us make it through the next week. Help us hang on until you split the eastern sky with trumpet sounds and we are snatched out of here. Amen."

This way of thinking is prevalent in Western Christianity, but unfortunately, it's not Biblical. A major function of the apostolic ministry, therefore, is to address these issues and straighten out false doctrine. Since God has restored apostles into the church, we are in the mode of doctrine-correcting. It is a challenge. Entire libraries have been filled with books teaching that Jesus came to earth to give us enough Holy Spirit that we could endure until we get our ticket "home" when he returns to rescue us.

How do we get free of false doctrine? Remember our four steps:

- Who said it?
- Who was it said to?

- What did it mean in the culture?
- How do we apply to our life?

False doctrine is not just errors in accuracy. It's rooted in lies. Now, I don't mean that the people teaching false doctrine are liars. They're not. Many are fine people doing their best with what they have. The tragedy is that what they have is embalmed with lies.

So, when we read:

Let them rule over the fish of the sea and over the birds of the sky and over the livestock and over all the earth, and over every crawling thing that crawls on the earth.

Genesis 1:26

We have to read this as God intended.

God was saying: "Let them rule over—*radah* over, *kingdom* over—all the earth. Every piece of creation."

Now comes the good part.

So God created man in His own image, in the image of God He created him; male and female He created them.

Genesis 1:27

We have another "them" here—*male and female!*

God blessed them; and God said to them, "Be fruitful and multiply, and fill the earth, and subdue it; and rule over the fish of the sea and over the birds of the sky and over every living thing that moves on the earth."

Genesis 1:28

God blessed mankind. Notice, however, that a blessing is different from a command. A blessing is an impartation. God, by creating man in his image and likeness, imparted to mankind the ability to *radah*—to govern—just as he does.

"God said to them..." God spoke this blessing. This is significant because God rules by his words. God was not merely bestowing a blessing over man, patting him on the head and cooing, "Oh, you're so cute." That's not blessing; that's a compliment. Here in Genesis, God was declaring a function within man. He was speaking the design of their DNA—who they are at their core. He was imparting not only an assignment, but the *identity* to fulfill the assignment.

That DNA is within us today. It is in the core of who we are. We are God's image and likeness. It drives everything we do in our lives.

So where does the misunderstanding come from? There is a significant mistranslation of Psalm 8:4-5 in the venerable King James Bible, one that affects how we view God's blessing on mankind. From the KJV:

What is man, that thou art mindful of him? and the son of man, that thou visitest him?

For thou hast made him <u>a little lower than the angels,</u> and hast crowned him with glory and honour.

First of all, who says "visitest" anymore? But second, this translation tells us that God made man *a little lower than the angels.* This is not correct. It is the wrong translation and the wrong theology.

The correct translation says it this way:

What is man that You think of him,
And a son of man that You are concerned about him?
Yet You have made him a little lower than God,
And You crown him with glory and majesty!

See the difference? We are a little lower than Elohim. Angels are not over us; they are under us. A study of Hebrews 1-2 confirms this.

God was specific in his instructions to man:

God blessed them; and God said to them, "Be fruitful and multiply, and fill the earth, and subdue it; and rule over the fish of the sea and over the birds of the sky and over every living thing that moves on the earth." Then God said, "Behold, I have given you every plant yielding seed that is on the surface of all the earth, and every tree which has fruit yielding seed; it shall be food for you; and to every animal of the earth and to every bird of the sky and to everything that moves on the earth which has life, I have given every green plant for food"; and it was so.

Notice that God never tells us to rule over one another. Nowhere in this original blessing does God say, "Go rule over your fellow man." Rather, he says, "Rule over all of creation."

Look at what God did when Israel asked him for a king. He tried his best to talk them out of it, but in the end, they persisted and so, he acquiesced.

Then all the elders of Israel gathered together and came to Samuel at Ramah; and they said to him, "Behold, you have grown old, and your sons do not walk in your ways. Now appoint us a king to judge us like all the nations." But the matter was displeasing in the sight of Samuel when they said, "Give us a king to judge us." And Samuel prayed to the Lord. And the Lord said to Samuel, "Listen to the voice of the people regarding all that they say to you, because they have not rejected you, but they have rejected Me from being King over them. Like all the deeds which they have done since the day that I brought them up from Egypt even to this day—in that they have abandoned Me and served other gods—so they are doing to you as well. Now then, listen to their voice; however, you shall warn them strongly and tell them of the practice of the king who will reign over them."

1 Samuel 8:4-9

It was not God's desire for Israel to have a king. He was their King. But Israel, from the remnants of an enslaved culture, wanted a man to rule over them. This started in the desert when they wanted Moses to stand between them and God. So, the Lord allowed it, although it wasn't his best. God wanted them to have *radah* (rule, dominion) upon the earth, operating in the sphere of influence that he created for them to function in. He wanted them to rule, but instead, they wanted to be ruled, so God allowed it.

A kingdom is made up of individuals; thus, the strength of the kingdom is found in the strength of each member. Like the Israelis of the Old Testament, we today are not intended to be ruled by man but to rule under the rulership of Almighty God. As a diverse body, God gave us gifts to rule different aspects of earth together in harmony as an extension of heaven on earth.

No individual is intended to rule over everything, but all of us together are intended to rule over all. God has given each of us our specific place in the culture to rule. And yet, exercising such rule is rare among mankind, even among Christians.

Social scientists tell us that 6% of people in any sphere of influence actually govern it. These are they who create the culture for that particular sphere. Only 6% rule it; the rest follow the rulers.

Our goal is to raise six-percenters. No, not six people we call "percenters," but countless people who will be the 6% of our population that governs. They do not seek jobs; they create jobs, and they change the culture of whatever they are a part of. In law enforcement, government, banking, construction, teaching, bus driving, garbage collecting, grave digging, septic cleaning or editing—it does not matter. They bring kingdom culture to their sphere of influence to transform it.

This is a radical idea. Most Christians in Western culture go to a sphere of influence with the idea of earning a living. Yet God never told us, "Go earn a living." Indeed, he said, "I will take care of all that."

Do not worry then, saying, 'What are we to eat?' or 'What are we to drink?' or 'What are we to wear for clothing?' For the Gentiles eagerly seek all these things; for your heavenly Father knows that you need all these things.

Matthew 6:31-32

Jesus was referring to everything people run after. What are they going to wear? What are they going to eat? What kind of house are they going to live in? These should not be our pursuit.

"Your pursuit," Jesus said, "should be the kingdom of God and righteousness." That is our pursuit.

But seek first His kingdom and His righteousness, and all these things will be provided to you.

Matthew 6:33

Notice where Jesus' words shift. "But..." That's one of those pivot words that nullifies all that came before it as it establishes a new principle. In redneck, it means "Shut up, sit up and listen. Stuff's about to get real."

"But seek first His kingdom." This word *first* in the Greek is the word *pro*, meaning "chief." Surprisingly, it means "first, before anything in front of, first of all."

First of all. First in importance. First things first. (Could it be any clearer?) Jesus was saying: "Before you do anything in your life, before anything else, seek first the kingdom—the king's dominion. The king's *radah*."

We say, "But that is Jesus'." No, no, no. That is yours. Seek the kingdom. The kingdom of Heaven.

Our job is to manifest the Kingdom of God. This word *seek* is the word *zeteo* in the Greek. It does not mean "look for, as it is lost." Rather, it means "to manifest it, to demand it, make it known, sought or see."

Consider how Jesus used the word in his message to Nicodemus:

Very truly I tell you, no one can see the kingdom of God unless they are born again.

John 3:3

Jesus told Nicodemus, "Look, you cannot *see* the kingdom of God unless you are born again." This does not refer to the eye alone. Rather, it means to "step into and participate, to manifest."

When God refers to "kingdom," it is not religion in any capacity. It is not white steeples and hymn books, choir robes and collection plates. It is not overheads, jumbotrons, amplifiers or speaker towers. It is government. When we say *kingdom* and *dominion*, we are saying *government. Radah* means government. Kingdom is government, nation or country.

When Jesus was questioned concerning kingdom, his reply mystified folks:

> *Now He was questioned by the Pharisees as to when the kingdom of God was coming, and He answered them and said, "The kingdom of God is not coming with signs that can be observed; nor will they say, 'Look, here it is!' or, 'There it is!' For behold, the kingdom of God is in your midst."*
>
> Luke 17:20-21

This word *midst* is the Greek word *entos* and it literally means "within; inside you." It denotes position in the Kingdom of God.

When Jesus said the Kingdom of God is near, he was saying the nation of God was near them; the government of God was near them; the country of God was near them.

> *Now no shrub of the field was yet on the earth, and no plant of the field had yet sprouted, for the LORD God had not sent rain upon the earth, and there was no man to cultivate the ground. But a mist used to rise from the earth and water the whole surface of the ground. Then the LORD God formed the man of dust from the ground, and breathed into his nostrils the breath of life; and the man became a living person. The LORD God planted a garden toward the east, in Eden; and there He placed the man whom He had formed. Out of the ground the LORD God caused every tree to grow that is pleasing to the sight and good for food...*
>
> Genesis 2:5-9

Consider the implications here. There was no man to cultivate the ground. This word *cultivate* sounds agricultural, but it is the Hebrew word *manage*. "To manage...to govern."

God did not let it rain because he did not have a man to manage the earth. God created the heavens and the earth and everything in the earth—all the shrubs, trees, bugs and elephants, everything on the earth. But God withheld rain because he did not want anything producing, growing and multiplying until he had a man on the earth.

God never designed the earth to *radah* itself. He designed man to *radah* the earth—to govern it. He gave them dominion. He gave him government on the earth. And the government that he gave them was not planting a garden. God already planted the garden.

> *The Lord God planted a garden toward the east, in Eden; and there He placed the man whom He had formed.*
>
> Genesis 2:8

God planted the garden and gave it to man.

> *Then the LORD God took the man and put him in the Garden of Eden to cultivate it and tend it.*
>
> Genesis 2:15

The Garden was just a piece of the earth; it was not the entirety of the earth, nor was man assigned only to the Garden. God placed man amongst the azaleas and water buffalo and said, "I want you to take what I have given you and expand it throughout the whole earth. The garden was a pilot project. It was not a place where man would hang out forever and say: "Oh wow, life is good. We're just going to walk with God in the cool of the day. And tomorrow we'll do the same thing. And forever."

In truth, the garden was the foundational seed from which man was to propagate throughout the earth.

Sometimes we get an idyllic image from this passage in Genesis 2:8:

> *Now they heard the sound of the Lord God walking in the garden in the cool of the day,*

Yet the phrase "cool of the day" literally means "to walk in the Spirit." So, we could read: "Adam walked with God in the Spirit." Cool, huh?

Romans 8:14 takes this further:

For all who are being led by the Spirit of God, these are sons and daughters of God.

Let's be clear on something. The word *son* in this context is not male. The word *son* in the Greek literally means "mature." It is in contrast to the word *child* which means "immature." So, ladies, if men can be the bride of Christ, you can be sons of God. We're all in this together.

As sons, we are "mature," walking in a place of partnership with God. That is why God never allowed the earth to do what was in his heart until he had man installed. Mankind's job was to have kingdom.

This is reflected in Jesus' purpose, from 1 John 3:8:

The one who practices sin is of the devil; for the devil has been sinning from the beginning. The Son of God appeared for this purpose, to destroy the works of the devil.

Jesus' purpose was to come and to get back what man gave away. He came to nullify the contract that Satan and Adam formed in the garden that wreaked havoc on the rest of the earth throughout generations.

But when the fullness of the time came, God sent His Son, born of a woman, born under the Law.

Galatians 4:4

Note, however, that Jesus' arrival was timed perfectly. The earth had been prepared to receive Jesus just as it had once been prepared for the arrival of Adam and Even. Both times, God withheld the rain until the perfect time—the rain of nature in the Garden and the rain of the Spirit upon the earth.

God always creates the atmosphere before he creates the product. He always builds the house before the inhabitants move in. He only sends the laborers when the fields are white with harvest. Consider:

- God created the sky before he created the bird.
- God created the water before he created the fish.

- God created the earth before he created the trees and plants.
- God created Eden before he created man.
- God created Adam before he created Eve.

Without the proper environment, the creature perishes. Take a bird out of the air, it becomes more vulnerable to its surroundings; most birds are safest in the air. Take a fish out of the water and it dies. Take up a tree out of the ground and it dies. Take a man out of Eden, and ...well, let's read what happens.

> The LORD God commanded the man, saying, "From any tree of the garden you may freely eat; but from the tree of the knowledge of good and evil you shall not eat, for on the day that you eat from it you will certainly die."
>
> Genesis 2:16-17

Obviously, Adam and Eve didn't die in a physical sense, so what did God mean by "you will certainly die"? He meant that after eating the fruit, God was going to pull him out of the Garden of Eden and place him in a foreign environment. Of course, the earth was placed in man's charge, so what was foreign about being removed from the garden? Simply this: The word *Eden* means "presence."

Presence. Think about it. The reason nobody can find Eden is because it is not a geographical location. It is an environment, an atmosphere, a spiritual location. In no sense does the word *Eden* mean "a plot of land." Rather, God put his presence in a certain place, then put man in that place on earth, and said, "Now, out of *this environment of Eden*, out of my presence, you can function and flow. You can multiply. You can subdue. You can be fruitful. You can *radah.*"

Take man out of Eden—God's presence—and he dies.

But...put man *back* into the presence of God and he thrives.

This was the foundation of man's creation, assignment and relationship with God.

So, we now understand that God created the heavens and the earth, put Adam with his presence (his Spirit, the "cool of the day"), and

Adam was to rule out of that. He was to *radah* out of that because the Spirit of God was there. Again, God's presence is the Holy Spirit.

So, Adam walked with the Spirit of the Lord, and he governed the earth according to the Lord's purpose. That purpose was to maintain the environment in which Adam could be what he was created to be. The Holy Spirit was there to help Adam govern by pointing Adam to the Father's heart.

For example, when God said: "Adam, look at all this creation. I want you to name all the animals. I want you to name all the herbs. I want you to name everything here on earth," understand that this was no guessing game. God was not saying: "Hey Adam, what do you think this is? It has a long, speckled neck and eats on the top of trees. Guess what it is, Adam? I'll give you a hint: it starts with 'G'."

That was not God's intent. God was saying: "Adam, I want you to name them all. But in so doing, I want you to do for them what I did for you."

What did God do for Adam? God spoke into Adam and blessed him, creating his identity. So, just as God had done, every time Adam named something, he was pulling its identity from the heart of God and speaking it into creation. Whatever Adam declared, it became. That's why an elephant is an elephant and a goose is a goose. Geese lay eggs and elephants don't fly. (Thank God for that!) When Adam spoke to a thing through the governance –the *radah*—of his words, the DNA of that thing captured the heart of God, and it became that thing. So, Adam was not merely assigning names to all the plants and animals; he was governing creation as God intended.

From Genesis 2:15,

> Then the Lord God took the man and put him in the Garden
> of Eden to cultivate it and tend it.

The expression "cultivate it and tend it" implies "to work it, manage it, rule it." Adam had purpose, duties, responsibilities. Quite a load, but he was not intended to do it alone.

*So the LORD God caused a deep sleep to fall upon the man,
and he slept; then He took one of his ribs and closed up the
flesh at that place.*

Genesis 2:21

What do you do when a subordinate is overwhelmed? You give him
a nap. God put Adam to sleep and he woke up with a strange woman
beside him. (The good news is they were married.) Still, he had to have
been startled:

*At last this is bone of my bones,
And flesh of my flesh;
She shall be called "woman,"
Because she was taken out of man.*

Genesis 2:23

The word *woman* literally means "womb man" or "man with a
womb." And remember that *man* refers to "mankind." So, Eve was "that
part of mankind that has a womb."

As happy as that occurrence was, dark clouds were forming on the
horizon. From Genesis 3:1-6

*Now the serpent was more cunning than any animal of the
field which the LORD God had made. And he said to the
woman, "Has God really said, 'You shall not eat from any tree
of the garden'?"*

*The woman said to the serpent, "From the fruit of the trees
of the garden we may eat; but from the fruit of the tree which
is in the middle of the garden, God has said, 'You shall not eat
from it or touch it, or you will die.'"*

*The serpent said to the woman, "You certainly will not die!
For God knows that on the day you eat from it your eyes will
be opened, and you will become like God, knowing good and
evil."*

*When the woman saw that the tree was good for food, and
that it was a delight to the eyes, and that the tree was*

desirable to make one wise, she took some of its fruit and ate;
and she also gave some to her husband with her, and he ate.

There was a dirty deal underway, a negotiation with evil being made. The enemy's proposition was this: "If you want to be like God, eat this fruit." Sounds friendly enough.

The problem was they were already like God.

So she ate. He ate. They sinned. And they fell.

Note that while the common term for this event is that mankind *fell*, that is not accurate. The best definition for what happened in the Garden is that mankind *sinned*. Sin is rebellion. So, mankind rebelled against God. They came under a contract with the enemy. They yielded their *radah*, and the enemy took their *radah*.

Remarkably, God never intervened. God never said, "Wait a minute, Lucifer. You are not doing that. You, devil, do not do that. You serpent, do not do that."

Why didn't God intervene?

Well, Adam had the authority in the earth. Adam had control. God had charge. That was the contract between God and man.

During the transaction, God said nothing. Yet he saw the whole thing. It's not like he was on vacation somewhere and returned home and cried, "What happened to my kingdom?"

Adam and Eve were in control. Yet they made a transaction with the enemy that transferred the *radah, the rule* into the hands of the enemy. God's position was: "Wait a minute. I did not do anything about it, but I can say something."

The devil forgot that God could talk. And when God talks, stuff happens. Here's part of what happened from Genesis 3:15:

And I will make enemies
Of you and the woman,
And of your offspring and her Descendant;
He shall bruise you on the head,
And you shall bruise Him on the heel.

Now, what does this mean? Remember our method of inquiry. Who said it? Who did they say it to? And what did it mean in their culture? Please understand that Adam and Eve did not write Genesis. Moses wrote it. So, what was the significance of the heel mentioned in the above passage?

In Hebrew culture, when a baby was born, they held the baby upside down and slapped the baby on the heel. And the baby would draw breath into its lungs. It is like in our Western culture when we slap the baby's bottom to get him to breathe at birth. So what God was saying through Moses in interpreting this particular historical acquisition was this: "You may have taken the kingdom, Satan, but this woman I created, I gave her a womb. I created a door into the earth before a door was ever needed. I made a way to re-enter the earth before I needed a way."

3

Reborn

IN JOHN 1, WE READ THAT IN THE BEGINNING, Jesus was the Word with God, and that through him all things were made. In 1 John 3:8, we are told that the purpose of Jesus appearing was to destroy the works of the devil. And finally, in Luke 4, we have Jesus' own words describing his purpose:

> *"I must also preach the kingdom of God to the other cities, because I was sent for this purpose."*

> Luke 4:43

Jesus came to earth to take back what Adam gave away—the Kings' dominion on the earth, which was not a religion but a government, a kingdom. God gave his word; because of the transaction that took place in the garden, he was going to send his Son and allow Jesus' life to be taken. But in the process, the authority of the enemy would be annihilated. Hence, the good news of the gospel.

In Luke 4:5, after Jesus was baptized in the Jordan river by John, he was tempted by the enemy. The temptations started with a grand display of what Jesus would get for serving Satan. (Sound familiar?)

> *And he led Him up and showed Him all the kingdoms of the world in a moment of time.*

Now the Greek word for *all* means "all, everything." In this case, all the kingdoms of the world shown in a moment's time. From Luke 4:6:

> *And the devil said to Him, "I will give You all this domain and its glory, for it has been handed over to me, and I give it to whomever I want.*

The essence of the bargain was this: "I will give you all these—kingdoms, domain, governments and the glory of these things." Remember, the word *glory* means "the weight of a thing, presence." So, we understand the glory of God as "the weight of God's glory, his presence, in a place." As stated earlier, mankind was created to operate out of the presence of God. This is the true meaning of Eden. So when Adam sinned, the presence of God was removed and another presence (or weight) stepped in. Glory is the weight of presence.

Satan's offer to Jesus was: "I'm going to give you all of the kingdoms, all of the rule of the world, *and* the weight of my presence, for it has been handed over to me."

Where were they handed over to him? In the Garden.

"I made a deal. I got them. A transaction was made. Everything on the earth that you see now is mine."

No, he did not say "the earth." He said "all that's in the earth, the world, all the rule, all of the government in the earth has been given to me. And I can give them to whomever I will."

Sweet deal, really, for the Son sent to be the savior of the world. Here it is offered up on a silver platter. No struggle, no cross, no pain or suffering. Just one catch. One little bitty stipulation.

Therefore if You worship before me [Satan], it shall all be Yours.

Luke 4:7

Now, what was the enemy's original plan? What was the thing that got him evicted from heaven? From Isaiah 14:13-14:

But you said in your heart,
"I will ascend to heaven;
I will raise my throne above the stars of God,
And I will sit on the mount of assembly
In the recesses of the north.
I will ascend above the heights of the clouds;
I will make myself like the Most High."

That was Satan's goal. So, man's transaction in the garden was not his final play. It was a deal leading to the big deal.

Of course, the enemy is not omniscient. He is not the evil equal of God's goodness. The enemy is an unemployed cherub; that's all he is. He slipped in and seized the kingdoms of the world. And in this moment recorded in Luke 4, he is seizing this opportune time with Jesus, the Son of God.

"Look, I know why You're here. But I tell you what, I'll give it all to you. Let's just save all the fuss. I'll give it all to you if you'll just bow down and worship me." Now this word *worship* is the word *proskuneo* in the Greek and it means, "to kiss or to kiss the ring, as in to kiss the ring of a ruler or a king."

That was Satan's plan the whole time. He wanted God to worship him, and if Jesus would have bowed down and worshiped him, Satan would have been exalted above God. Therein lied the method to his madness. Thankfully, Jesus rejected his proposal.

I DID IT GOD'S WAY

There is a lesson for all of us here. We cannot illegitimately obtain the things we know God wants us to have and prosper in. God's blessings have to come God's way. Blessings require qualification. Often, the promise of a blessing is made to lead us on the path that prepares us to receive those things. Shortcutting that process actually empowers the devil in our lives and puts us on the path to perdition.

It's possible that Adam and Eve would have eventually been offered the Tree of the Knowledge of Good and Evil, and even the Tree of Life. We don't know. God must have had a purpose in placing those trees in the Garden. However, their fruit was certainly not for man at that time...and his disobedience cost him and the human race dearly. When we trade things that are eternal for things that are temporal, we give up our inheritance.

Both man and Jesus were tempted in similar ways. So, whose example should we follow? Jesus', of course! Jesus' response to each temptation was clear: "It is written...."

The Devil did not have a cloven hoof to stand on.

Of course, we might be tempted to cut Adam and Eve some slack. Afterall, nothing had been written at the time of the Garden, right?

Well...wrong. When Jesus said "It is written..." he wasn't talking about the Old Testament. He was talking about the purpose, plan and intent of God's heart as manifested throughout the law and the prophets. Jesus had the Word written in his heart; the same word expressed through the writers of the Old Testament. Remember: "In the beginning was the Word...."

Recall why Jesus came to earth. It says in Hebrews 10:5-7:

Therefore, when He comes into the world, He says,

"You have not desired sacrifice and offering,

But You have prepared a body for Me;

You have not taken pleasure in whole burnt offerings and offerings for sin.

Then I said, 'Behold, I have come

(It is written of Me in the scroll of the book)

To do Your will, O God.'"

For Satan, this isn't about the kingdoms of the world; this is about worship.

"Satan, you want to be exalted above my God, my Father? Well, I'm not worshiping you. I only worship God and He says I'm going to get what you're offering me, but I'm going to get it His way. I'm coming after you to take back the kingdom you are offering. So, I'm not in a deal-making mood today."

Satan thought he had a regular ole man. But he had the new man standing before him. And when Jesus refused to make this deal to get what the Father sent him after—the kingdoms, dominion and government of the world—Satan tried to get Jesus to kill himself. Yet Jesus' approach was firm: "I want these things, but I'm going to get them legitimately—the Father's way!"

Jesus did not come to earth in search of religion. This is why Satan did not offer Jesus a temple. Jesus came after a kingdom, and his purpose was to destroy the works of the devil.

> *The one who practices sin is of the devil; for the devil has been sinning from the beginning. The Son of God appeared for this purpose, to destroy the works of the devil.*

1 John 3:8

> *But He said to them, "I must also preach the kingdom of God to the other cities, because I was sent for this purpose."*

Luke 4:43

We see clearly what Adam gave away in the Garden when, in Luke 4, the enemy tries to negotiate with the Son of God by offering all the kingdoms of the world if Jesus will worship him. Jesus, the sinless son of God, said "No deal."

Now, we understand what was at stake. Jesus did not come to establish or fix a religion. He came for a kingdom. We know what Jesus thought of religion and temples from his discussion with his disciples on the Mount of Olives.

> *Jesus left the temple area and was going on His way when His disciples came up to point out the temple buildings to Him. But He responded and said to them, "Do you not see all these things? Truly I say to you, not one stone here will be left upon another, which will not be torn down."*

Matthew 24:1-2

Now, that's not good news. We know that it was Jesus saying this, but who was he saying it to? The Jews. The entirety of their lives was wrapped up in that temple, and this upstart, this religious nobody, publicly declared that it would be destroyed. No doubt, the disciples recalled Jesus early words (recorded in John 2:18-20).

The Jews then said to Him, "What sign do You show us as your authority for doing these things?" Jesus answered them, "Destroy this temple, and in three days I will raise it up." The Jews then said, "It took forty-six years to build this temple, and yet You will raise it up in three days?"

Of course, Jesus was referring to this body, but at the time, nobody knew that. At this time in history, everything the Jewish nation stood for, its history and its future, was tied into that temple. So fixated were they on the temple and what it represented that even after his resurrection (but before Pentecost), Jesus disciples asked:

So, when they had come together, they began asking Him, saying, "Lord, is it at this time that You are restoring the kingdom to Israel?"

Acts 1:6

Jesus' message, paraphrased, was this: "I've not come to put a new patch on an old garment. I'm not here to fix your broken religious system. I'm not into old wineskins because they will burst and the wine will be spilled. I've come to give you a new and living way. I am the resurrection and the life."

JESUS' MESSAGE

Jesus came talking about Kingdom. In fact, this is the only message Jesus ever preached.

Read through the gospels and find where Jesus preached the gospel of prosperity. He never did, did he? Instead, prosperity followed him everywhere he went. When he needed money, money was there. When Jesus needed to pay his taxes, he said to Peter: "I know you're used to fishing with a net but get a pole. (I can just picture Peter hunting for a cane pole.) You throw the line and the first fish you catch, look in his mouth and there'll be a coin. Go pay your taxes and pay mine too." (I have always wondered what bait Peter used.)

Remarkably, Jesus didn't preach the gospel of healing either. He just healed whoever came to him. It came out of Him. He preached the Kingdom and healing manifested.

Jesus never preached the gospel of deliverance. Jesus did not have a deliverance ministry. Deliverance just happened wherever he put his foot on the ground. Everywhere the king took steps, there was the kingdom.

> *Every place on which the sole of your foot steps, I have given it to you, just as I spoke to Moses.*

> Joshua 1:3

Jesus was in a boat and came ashore at the Land of the Gerasenes. A demon-possessed man ran to Jesus and fell at his feet saying "What business do You have with me, Jesus, Son of the most high God? I beg You, do not torment me!" (Luke 8:28). This was the enemy engaging in classic negotiation techniques, trying to make a deal where there was no deal. Notice the power Jesus had over these demons.

> *And Jesus asked him, "What is your name?" And he said, "Legion"; because many demons had entered him. And they were begging Him not to command them to go away into the abyss.*

> Luke 8:30-31

The devils were trying to cut a deal. And what did Jesus do? He cast the devils out of the man and sent them into a nearby herd of pigs— demon-possessed bacon! And the pigs rushed down a steep bank, headlong into a lake and were drowned.

This, of course, incurred another problem, since the pigs were owned by local Jews who were not supposed to have anything to do with these unclean animals. Still, they became incensed at Jesus for interrupting their business, illegal as it was, and eventually the town fell under great fear and asked Jesus to leave, which he did. God never stays where he is not wanted.

Yes, Jesus had a deliverance ministry, but it was because he carried kingdom authority. Deliverance is not a spiritual act; it's a supernatural act. There's a difference. When you cast demons out of someone, you are evicting them from God's land. In a sense, the possessed person is God's property and the demons are trespassing. The legal rights are clear—you have the right; the demons do not. It's a legal transaction that gets the job done, not a show. You don't have to dress up in a bow tie, scream in tongues, and dance in the Spirit to get a demon out. All you have to do is speak. No need to crank up the Hammond B3, assemble the choir, or have fifty ladies fanning themselves to pass out in the aisle.

Deliverance is the exercise of governmental authority, not a religious experience.

SAVE ME!

Now, this will shake things up. Jesus never preached the gospel of Salvation either. Jesus only spoke of being born-again one time and that was in the middle of the night talking to a Pharisee named Nicodemus, a man who had come to him in secret.

> *Now there was a man of the Pharisees, named Nicodemus, a ruler of the Jews; this man came to Jesus at night and said to Him, "Rabbi, we know that You have come from God as a teacher; for no one can do these signs that You do unless God is with him." Jesus responded and said to him, "Truly, truly, I say to you, unless someone is born again he cannot see the kingdom of God."*

John 3:1-3

Jesus just gave this man the essence of his message, and it was not about getting into heaven or getting demons out or hitting the jackpot. It was about getting into the Kingdom of God.

Now, I realize this gets some precious pigs rushing toward the cliff, but we've got to understand. Who is Jesus talking to in this passage?

What do the words mean in their culture? And how do we apply to our life?

Jesus was telling Nicodemus: "Unless you are born again, you cannot see the Kingdom of God." This word *see* in the Greek is *horao*, meaning "to perceive or to attend to." Most people see, but to perceive is more than see. To *perceive* literally means "to possess the knowledge of something, to own that piece of it."

Jesus was saying that if you want to see the kingdom, if you want to perceive it, you're going to have to be born again.

Jesus answered, "Truly, truly, I say to you, unless someone is born of water and the Spirit, he cannot enter the kingdom of God. That which has been born of the flesh is flesh, and that which has been born of the Spirit is spirit. Do not be amazed that I said to you, 'You must be born again.' The wind blows where it wishes, and you hear the sound of it, but you do not know where it is coming from and where it is going; so is everyone who has been born of the Spirit."

John 3:5-8

For all who are being led by the Spirit of God, these are sons and daughters of God.

Romans 8:14

Jesus is describing a relationship with the Father, one born of water and spirit, a new birth.

BORN OF WATER

Now, some folks think that being born of water refers to a human birth because a woman's water breaks as part of her labor. Still, this is not what Jesus was talking about.

To understand Jesus' statement to Nicodemus in John 3, we must go back to Jesus' cousin, John the Baptist. John was the forerunner of Christ. The Bible calls him a prophet. It also says that his father was the high priest, meaning John was in line for that position. But John did not pursue his father's path. Addressing the Pharisees and Sadducees, he said:

> *"As for me, I baptize you with water for repentance, but He who is coming after me is mightier than I, and I am not fit to remove His sandals; He will baptize you with the Holy Spirit and fire. His winnowing fork is in His hand, and He will thoroughly clear His threshing floor; and He will gather His wheat into the barn, but He will burn up the chaff with unquenchable fire."*

> Matthew 3:11-12

When Adam sinned, the Holy Spirit left him and Adam no longer governed the earth by his words. Instead, he governed by his hands. The Bible tells us Adam had to till the ground with his hands.

> *Then to Adam He said, "Because you have listened to the voice of your wife, and have eaten from the tree about which I commanded you, saying, 'You shall not eat from it';*
>
> *Cursed is the ground because of you;*
> *With hard labor you shall eat from it*
> *All the days of your life.*
> *Both thorns and thistles it shall grow for you;*
> *Yet you shall eat the plants of the field;*
> *By the sweat of your face*
> *You shall eat bread,*
> *Until you return to the ground,*
> *Because from it you were taken;*
> *For you are dust,*
> *And to dust you shall return."*

> Genesis 3:17-19

The earth could no longer respond to Adams words. Now he had to coerce it by forced labor. The earth was outside the creative kingdom purpose that God intended for it because there was another presence, another weight there—that of the enemy.

From that time on, the spirit of God never filled anyone until John in the womb of his mother, Elizabeth. The Bible says Holy Spirit came upon various people for tasks, assignments, and spiritual perspective (like Elisha seeing the spiritual army around him and Elijah. (ref. 2 Kings 2:12). But Holy Spirit never lived in a human until John, and John's message was this: "The Messiah, Yeshua, is coming and he will bring back the Spirit of God that was in the garden, returning the cool of the day. He's going to reposition us in God."

John preached "Repent, for the Kingdom of Heaven is at hand." He never preached religion; he had nothing to do with religion. Kingdom is government, nation, country. Just "repent."

Interesting word, *repent*. It does not mean "confess" as in:

If we confess our sins, He is faithful and righteous, so that He will forgive us our sins and cleanse us from all unrighteousness.

1 John 1:9

When we confess our sins, God forgives us and cleanses us, but confession is not repentance. It's not merely acknowledging sin in our lives. People often come to church thinking they need to confess their sins to the Lord. That's a good start, but *repent* goes further. It means: "to change the way that you think, the way that you relate to, or the way that you have purposed something." It is the Greek word *metanoia*.

Remember our line of inquiry. When John said to repent for the Kingdom of God is hand, who was he talking to? Was he talking to Gentiles? No, because Jesus came first to the Jews and then the Gentiles.

John's message to the Jewish people to repent meant to change the way that they think, the way they relate to God, and the way they purpose God. This radical new word was upending their religion and wrecking their lives.

John was saying to the Jewish nation: "Look, you related to God in the temple, but God is saying 'repent for the Kingdom of God is at hand.'

There is a kingdom, there is a dominion of sovereignty that is at hand right now. And there's one coming after me who will baptize you with Holy Spirit and fire. And when he does, the Father is going to come back into your life, but it will not be like that temple. There'll be no more sacrificing animals. It's time to change the way you think about God. REPENT!"

It's helpful to realize that when the Word refers to *heart*, it's not talking about that thing beating in your chest. It's literally referring to your subconscious mind where everything about your life and what you believe is stored. This is what Paul meant when he said to the Roman church:

> *Therefore I urge you, brothers and sisters, by the mercies of God, to present your bodies as a living and holy sacrifice, acceptable to God, which is your spiritual service of worship. And do not be conformed to this world, but be transformed by the renewing of your mind, so that you may prove what the will of God is, that which is good and acceptable and perfect.*
>
> *For through the grace given to me I say to everyone among you not to think more highly of himself than he ought to think; but to think so as to have sound judgment, as God has allotted to each a measure of faith.*
>
> Romans 12:1-3

So renewal involves relearning, rethinking, repenting, ridding ourselves of religion and receiving the Kingdom of God. Hence John's message to repent and be baptized.

Now, John was a prophet, but he was also a rabbi just as Jesus was. There were many rabbis in that area. *Rabbi* is the Jewish word that means "master teacher." It is not a prophet or a priest. It doesn't mean apostle or pastor. It means "master teacher, one who is a master in a school of thought."

John's ministry, then, was propagating a school of thought. It wasn't the school of thought that was being taught in the temple. They were teaching religion—the Jewish religion. John was propagating the Kingdom of God. This master teacher was in the wilderness teaching these people that the Kingdom of God was coming and they had to be ready to change their thinking. John could just as well have said "Prepare for the renewal of your minds. I'm your master teacher. If you adhere to my message, there's a way you can show it." We call it the outward manifestation.

Historically, every master teacher had a way for people to identify publicly with their message. John's way was baptism; others had different methods. You can read Jewish history by the historian Josephus. Many other ways were used by other master teachers; some even declared themselves to be the Christ at the time Jesus was on the earth.

The way you got baptized back then was to walk into the water, identify that you adhere to the message of the Kingdom of God, and go under. (Hopefully you came back up.) Your baptism was certified by John as a witness; thousands of people were identified with the kingdom message. "Hey, Ebenezer just switched. He's no longer going to *do* the temple. Now he's going to *be* the temple." Big difference!

THE LAMB OF GOD

So one day, John's preaching his message and baptizing folks, and all of a sudden he stops and sees someone coming.

> Then Jesus arrived from Galilee at the Jordan, coming to John to be baptized by him. But John tried to prevent Him, saying, "I have the need to be baptized by You, and yet You are coming to me?" But Jesus, answering, said to him, "Allow it at this time; for in this way it is fitting for us to fulfill all righteousness." Then he allowed Him. After He was baptized, Jesus came up immediately from the water; and behold, the heavens were opened, and he saw the Spirit of God descending as a dove and settling on Him, and behold, a voice from the heavens said, "This is My beloved Son, with whom I am well pleased."

Matthew 3:13-17

Jesus walked into the river and said "John, baptize me. I need to be baptized by you."

Now, remember: Who said it? Who is he talking to? What did it mean in their culture?

John said, "No, I must be baptized by you."

Jesus said, "No, I must be baptized by you that the scriptures may be fulfilled."

What was the purpose of Jesus' baptism? The same as the other people being baptized. Jesus was identifying with the message that John was preaching as a master teacher. He was telling John, "Look, you have to baptize me so that whenever you're gone, people will know that I'm preaching the same message you preached."

Jesus was not baptized for the repentance of sins. He had none. Rather, he was making a public profession that he was adhering to what John preached and John baptized him.

It was not long after that that John was taken into custody. Matthew 4:17 says:

From that time Jesus began to preach and say, "Repent, for the kingdom of heaven is at hand."

Jesus began to preach the same message that John preached. Jesus became a rabbi, a master teacher in that region, and he began to preach the same message as John.

Folks, we are not baptized to get to heaven. We are baptized for the same reason Jesus was baptized: acknowledging that we are adhering to the message of the Kingdom of God and will forsake all but the message. It means we've left religion and are coming into a new country and a new government. Our home country has become the Kingdom of Heaven, and from that point on we don't preach the gospel of healing, deliverance, prosperity or salvation. We do not even preach religion. We preach the Kingdom of God, just as Jesus preached. And everything else will manifest.

4

Kingdom Dynamics

PEOPLE OFTEN USE THE TERMS KINGDOM OF HEAVEN AND KINGDOM OF GOD as though they are synonymous. In fact, they are related but refer to different aspects of God's rule. The Kingdom of Heaven is the governed territory of God. It is an entire sphere fully under God's authority and conforming to the law and order of the King of Heaven. The Kingdom of God, simply put, is the influence of the Kingdom of Heaven on earth.

The heavens were created for God to govern, and he created the earth for mankind to govern. So, the Kingdom of Heaven is the home country. It is where God dwells; it is where everything is under his dominion. He has 100% control in heaven. Everything conforms to his law and order of who he is—the King of Heaven.

In governmental terms, it's like Washington, D.C., where the federal government for the United States of America is based. It is where the full authority of the government of the United States resides. Whenever the United States government wants to expand its influence into other territories, it builds a federal building in that new territory. That federal building houses federal court, federal law enforcement and other things pertaining to the federal government in Washington, D.C. That federal building is under the influence of Washington, D.C. in that region, but it is not Washington, D.C. itself. Instead, it is tied to Washington, D.C. and all of its power and authority.

So, the Kingdom of Heaven is like Washington, D.C. to us. That is where the President resides. Everything that is done in our States is first legislated there, debated there and becomes law there. The President signs all laws there, and then they can be facilitated to the states and down to the county level. Most counties have federal buildings.

Likewise, everything that God wants done on the earth is first done in heaven. That is why Jesus taught us to pray:

Your kingdom come.
Your will be done,
On earth as it is in heaven.

Matthew 6:10

In essence, Jesus was saying: "Let the King's sovereignty and majesty be done in the earth from his dominion and authority in heaven. Not only his Kingdom come but his will be done. Let us not just have a federal building on earth, but let us have the will within that building to facilitate to all the citizens in that county everything that heaven wants."

So, the Kingdom on the earth is the territory of God. We are a colony of Heaven. God literally wants to colonize the earth, but we rebelled. It was an ugly, horrible thing. We changed citizenships. We sinned against our version of King George (King of England at the time of America's independence). We declared our independence but not in a righteous way. Adam sinned. He rebelled against the home country, declaring his independence from a righteous God and aligning with an unemployed cherub. We went under a new and nefarious governor.

Now, a governor of a colony is never from the colony. King George, for example, did not raise up people from the original 13 colonies to govern those territories. Instead, all of the King's governors came from England. Why? Because they understood the intent of King George for those colonies. They knew what King George wanted, and when they arrived and established rule, they strove to ensure that the Crown got everything it wanted.

Unfortunately, this foreign intervention started a rebellion in the hearts of the colonialists. They formed a continental army, a continental congress, and thus, in time, began the Revolutionary War.

This, in a sense, is what happened with Adam and Eve. Their rebellion was not religious, it was governmental. Consider the words used to seduce Eve, and by association, her husband, Adam:

Now the serpent was more cunning than any animal of the field which the Lord God had made. And he said to the woman, "Has God really said, 'You shall not eat from any tree of the garden'?" The woman said to the serpent, "From the fruit of the trees of the garden we may eat; but from the fruit of the tree which is in the middle of the garden, God has said, 'You shall not eat from it or touch it, or you will die.'" The serpent said to the woman, "You certainly will not die! For God knows that on the day you eat from it your eyes will be opened, and you will become like God, knowing good and evil."

Genesis 3:1-5

The serpent's challenge was not to God's rule in a religious sense. The challenge was to God's governmental authority, and from there, to man's governorship of the colony.

The rebellion in the garden was an attack on a colony—the Kingdom of God. Of course, some would still argue that man's fall in the Garden was of a religious nature. The reality, however, is that man's actions were in no capacity religious, but we have made it religious through our ignorance.

"Are you a religious man, Greg?"

"Oh, God, I hope not."

I can think of a lot of things I would rather be called—some of which might be true. But religious? No!

I am a government man, a kingdom man. My title on the earth—indeed the title of any believer—is *Ambassador*. That is a governmental term. It is the language of the Bible.

Nowhere in scripture does God call us Christians. The word *Christian* is recorded twice in the Bible, both times in Acts, and the historical context is revealing. The term *Christian* was not meant as a compliment. Rather, it was a derogatory term hurled towards sons and daughters of God. In a mocking way, it referred to believers as "little Christs."

Sometimes I wonder if we have advanced much further in the last two millenniums. Christianity today seems like a bunch of religious people struggling to make it to heaven by the skin of their teeth. In terms of ideology, philosophy and theology, Christianity as practiced today is nothing more than any another religion. It's time to break Christianity open by living as God intended us to live—operating in his power, bearing his likeness and walking in his light.

We must emerge from categories that the Father never assigned to us. I'm not saying to stop calling ourselves Christians. I am saying start living like believers—sons and daughters of God, anointed ones.

So much divides us: Methodist, Presbyterian, Catholic, Charismatic, Pentecostal. We separate by theology: post-trib, pre-trib, no-trib. We isolate by experience: tongues, no tongues, healing, no healing, miracles, no miracles. We stand apart in practice: stand, kneel, wine, grape juice, audience, congregation, amplifiers, acoustic. It's as if we invent things to establish our identity and then fight amongst ourselves to prove we are right (and the other folks are wrong).

If what we have accomplished since the third century in Christianity had worked, we'd be done by now.

The answers come from Jesus' words, understood through our questions in inquiry: Who said it? Who were they talking to? How did it fit in their culture? How does it apply to our lives today?

In this way, we can acquire the picture of what Jesus is doing, where he is leading and what is he assigning. We begin to see clearly as we read his words without the filter of Western Christianity. By understanding what God was saying in those particular cultures, we gain a much clearer picture of what the Father is saying to us today.

The Kingdom of Heaven is where everything originates. The Kingdom of God is the influence of the Kingdom of Heaven on earth. God wants to colonize the earth. That word, *colonize*, is what God meant when he told Adam to be fruitful and multiply, to subdue, to create, to expand the earth. It refers to the extension of a kingdom's influence into a distant territory.

> *God blessed them; and God said to them, "Be fruitful and multiply, and fill the earth, and subdue it; and rule over the fish of the sea and over the birds of the sky and over every living thing that moves on the earth."*
>
> Genesis 1:28

God wants to colonize our planet. He wants to extend his kingdom influence into this place called earth. This makes sense as long as we are reading with a governmental, kingdom lens. We lose this meaning when we read with a religious or denominational lens. Let us think like ambassadors. This is the essence of everything Jesus taught in Matthew 16.

> *Now when Jesus came into the region of Caesarea Philippi, He was asking His disciples, "Who do people say that the Son of Man is?" And they said, "Some say John the Baptist; and others, Elijah; and still others, Jeremiah, or one of the other prophets." He said to them, "But who do you yourselves say that I am?" Simon Peter answered, "You are the Christ, the Son of the living God."*
>
> *And Jesus said to him, "Blessed are you, Simon Barjona, because flesh and blood did not reveal this to you, but My Father who is in heaven.*
>
> Matthew 16:13-17

The key question here, the inquiry that opened God's revelation to the disciples, was simply this: "Who do you yourselves say that I am?"

Now, I love Peter. That boy kept his foot in his mouth more than any other disciple. But that day, Peter got it right.

"You are the Christ, the Son of the living God."

Now, who said it? Peter, obviously.

What did it mean in their culture? When Peter said: "You are the Christ, the son of the living God," it literally meant, "You are here about your father's business."

Remember what Jesus said when he was 12 years old and his parents found him in the temple?

Then, after three days they found Him in the temple, sitting in the midst of the teachers, both listening to them and asking them questions. And all who heard Him were amazed at His understanding and His answers.

When Joseph and Mary saw Him, they were bewildered; and His mother said to Him, "Son, why have You treated us this way? Behold, Your father and I have been anxiously looking for You!" And He said to them, "Why is it that you were looking for Me? Did you not know that I had to be in My Father's house?"

Luke 2:46-49

Yes, Jesus was in the temple, but he was not preaching the Jewish religion. He had already learned everything that he needed to learn by 12 years old. Rather, he was talking to the Jewish leaders about the kingdom. They were not astonished at how much he knew about their religion; that was standard training for a Jewish boy. They were astonished about what else he knew.

I encourage you to read Josephus' book of Jewish history. Josephus was a historian who was hired by Rome to write the history of the Jews. You will find all of these stories with greater explanation of how that transpired culturally.

In Bible college, Josephus was required reading to understand the history and culture of the Jewish people. If we had just read the Bible from our Western viewpoint, we would have infused all of our bias into our understanding. But knowing the culture of the day through a historian brought the scriptures into proper perspective.

Yes, we have Holy Spirit to teach us, yet we tend to pour what Holy Spirit gives us through our filters. God cannot give us things we are not equipped to receive. He could reveal to me the next great procedure for brain surgery, for example, but unless I'm trained as a brain surgeon, (I'm not, by the way, so don't ask), I'm not going to get it. Even in theology, a field I am trained in, God can only lead me into places I am prepared for. Oh, he still startles my mind at times, but I must be prepared to have my mind expanded. Unless the ground is properly prepared, the sower sows in vain.

Consider the key exchange in Matthew 16:

Peter: "You are the Christ, the Son of the living God."

Jesus: "Blessed are you, Simon Barjona, because flesh and blood did not reveal this to you, but My Father who is in heaven."

Now, where is Jesus looking when he responded to Peter's declaration? The clue is in Jesus' phrase "My Father." Recall that Jesus frequently associated the Father with his geographical location—heaven. "Our Father who is *in heaven*..." (Matthew 6:9). So, Jesus is looking toward heaven when he addresses Peter's revelation.

Why did Jesus do that? Why was it important for the disciples to know Father's location? Because heaven is the place from which the Father rules. And by association, it is the place from which they were to rule. Now the rest of Jesus' words take on new meaning:

> *And I also say to you that you are Peter, and upon this rock I will build My church; and the gates of Hades will not overpower it. I will give you the keys of the kingdom of heaven; and whatever you bind on earth shall have been bound in heaven, and whatever you loose on earth shall have been loosed in heaven."*

> Matthew 16:18-19

What was established here? The disciples knew who Jesus was— the Messiah. They also knew who revealed that truth to them—the Father *in heaven*. Now they could be instructed on the source of their rulership, their power. Jesus, the Son of the Father. The Father who is in heaven. Heaven, the seat of power for the Kingdom of God on earth. Point, set, match, Nike endorsement.

Yet after this tremendous revelation, one that likely left the disciples reeling, Jesus warned them to tell no one that he was the Christ, the Messiah.

> *Then He gave the disciples strict orders that they were to tell*
> *no one that He was the Christ.*

Matthew 16:20

No one? You reveal that you are the Messiah, and we can't tell a soul? Why did Jesus issue such a strict warning?

The answer is in the question: What did *Messiah* mean in their culture? Did the Jews expect the Messiah to establish a religion? No. They already had a religion, one originated from the law and the prophets. In fact, the Jews were expecting the Messiah to come and set up a kingdom, not a religion. They used the word *government*. In their minds, this Messiah, when he came and established his new government, would overthrow whatever government was ruling Israel and the Jews. So, they were not looking for a religious leader for themselves. They were looking for a Messiah, a King, to come and to save them from their oppressors.

Even after Jesus' resurrection, returning Israel to its former glory was chief in the minds of the disciples. Indeed, the very last thing they asked him before he ascended was this:

> *So, when they had come together, they began asking Him,*
> *saying, "Lord, is it at this time that You are restoring the*
> *kingdom to Israel?"*

Acts 1:6

EKKLESIA

When we view Jesus' ministry without the filter of religion, we arrive at kingdom. We can only understand his ministry and his impact on the Jews through a kingdom perspective. When Jesus said: "Upon this rock I will build My church," he was telling his disciples: "I am coming and I will build my church, my ekklesia."

The word *church* is not a religious word. We make it religious in our concepts when we use phrases such as: "We go to church." That just means we are going to a building where some preacher revs us up every Sunday so we can get through the rest of the week.

That building is not the church. That building is merely four walls, a roof and a steeple. And if you're lucky, some nice stained-glass windows to look at while you wait for lunchtime. The structure is the place where the church meets, but the church can meet anywhere. Jesus said as much:

> *For where two or three have gathered together in My name [Jesus], I am there in their midst."*

Matthew 18:20

The word *church* is the word *ekklesia*. It is not a religious word; it is a governmental word, and the disciples knew what that word meant in their culture. I'm sure their mouths dropped when they heard it. "Why is he using *ekklesia*? Why is he speaking about *church* so often? Has he been talking to Greg Hood?"

The Greek word *ekklesia* in their culture referred to the elders who gathered at the city gate to govern the affairs of the city. Among other things, the elders held authority over what could come and go through the city gates. They were the governors of the gates, the law, the leaders of the city. When major decisions were to be made, they rang a bell and all the citizens gathered as the elders led the city in major decisions such as going to war, assessing taxes, and which cities to align with. That was the word *church* as Jesus used it here.

The Romans took *ekklesia* a bit further, and it was this definition that Jesus was using because the Romans inhabited Israel at this time and greatly influenced its culture. God's timing, it seems, was perfect.

Recall Galatians 4: 4-5:

But when the fullness of the time came, God sent His Son, born of a woman, born under the Law, so that He might redeem those who were under the Law, that we might receive the adoption as sons and daughters.

The phrase "the fullness of time" refers to a time of maturation, a time when there was a model on the earth that closely resembled what God had in heaven. Jesus' use of the Roman *ekklesia* indicated there was a role model operating that closely resembled what the Father desired on the earth.

The Romans were warriors, fighters, conquerors and administrators. When they conquered a city, they sent an ekklesia—governors—into that city from Rome. Their assignment was to change the culture: the language, the food, the clothing, the architecture, the customs and laws. That is why you see Roman architecture in places like Israel. Everywhere the Romans went, they built buildings, renamed cities and streets, and changed currency. Most importantly, they changed the laws because Roman law produced Roman culture. Consequently, everywhere you went in the Roman empire, you found Roman culture. Everything looked, acted and felt like Rome.

Jesus, speaking to his disciples as the now-revealed Messiah, was saying: "I am going to build a kingdom patterned similar to Rome. I'm going to do it the same way, only with my ekklesia, my legislative arm. I am going to send my ekklesia. They are going to be culture changers. And the gates of Hades will not overpower it."

Now, when Rome sent an ekklesia to a region, they often did it with ships because of the vast distances to be covered. The ships brought everything necessary to facilitate culture change. And interestingly, they usually sent a flotilla of five ships. Five...

So Rome's ecclesia traveled in groups of five. What else travels in groups of five?

And He gave some as apostles, some as prophets, some as evangelists, some as pastors and teachers, for the equipping of the saints for the work of ministry, for the building up of the body of Christ.

Ephesians 4:11-12

Yes, the five-fold ministry of Jesus, the head of the ekklesia. Apostles, prophets, evangelists, pastors and teachers.

Coincidentally, the center ship of the Roman flotilla that led that group was called the Apostle ship. (Not "the Apostleship," but "the Apostle ship.") That was the ship that carried the governmental structure of Rome into the city.

Of course, some people today think *apostle* is a religious term. Weren't there 12 original apostles in Jesus' earthly ministry? Yes, but they were not religious, not in any capacity. *Apostle* is a Roman word pertaining to "one who is sent; to cause the establishment of a government." So when we say *apostle*, we are not talking about a religious leader but rather a governmental representation. It is expressed in a person but also should be expressed in the people.

Jesus' recognition of the prevailing Roman system was also evident in his answer to the Pharisees when they asked him about taxes:

Then they sent some of the Pharisees and Herodians to Him in order to trap Him in a statement. They came and said to Him, "Teacher, we know that You are truthful and do not care what anyone thinks; for You are not partial to anyone, but You teach the way of God in truth. Is it permissible to pay a poll-tax to Caesar, or not? Are we to pay, or not pay?" But He, knowing their hypocrisy, said to them, "Why are you testing Me? Bring Me a denarius to look at." And they brought one. And He said to them, "Whose image and inscription is this?" And they said to Him, "Caesar's." And Jesus said to them, "Pay to Caesar the things that are Caesar's, and to God the things that are God's." And they were utterly amazed at Him.

Mark 12:13-17

Why did Jesus respond this way? Because Roman coin was the currency in Jerusalem.

Folks, we are called to do the same thing in every area of society—bring his government, which is the government of the Kingdom of God—in line with the Kingdom of Heaven and change culture. We are here to change everything, everywhere we go. See, religion says that Jesus came to get us ready for heaven, but kingdom says Jesus came for us to occupy earth, just as the Father intended in the Garden.

Be fruitful and multiply, and fill the earth, and subdue it;

Genesis 1:28

Subdue means "to occupy."

When we think kingdom, it takes our focus off of heaven, and that is totally upsetting to religious people. Yet Jesus' intention was never for us to focus on heaven, but to focus on changing the culture of the colony of earth to mirror heaven. We are not being prepared to enter heaven. That is religion. Rather, we are preparing the earth to receive heaven. That is kingdom.

Your kingdom come.
Your will be done,
On earth as it is in heaven.

Matthew 16:10

5

Purposed for Use

ONE OF THE MOST POPULAR VERSES IN THE SCRIPTURE is John 3:16.

> *For God so loved the world, that He gave His only Son, so that everyone who believes in Him will not perish, but have eternal life.*

That was the first verse I learned as a good Baptist boy. I heard it preached every week in the churches my granddaddy used to take me to. He was what they called a county missionary. He oversaw all the churches in the county for the Southern Baptist Organization in Monroe County, Mississippi. I loved to go with him. Everywhere we went, I always heard it preached.

This scripture holds the keys to understanding kingdom. To see this, however, we need to review 1 John 3:8:

> *The one who practices sin is of the devil; for the devil has been sinning from the beginning. The Son of God appeared for this purpose, to destroy the works of the devil.*

Jesus' purpose was to destroy the works of the devil. And that harkens back to the Garden, to Adam's rebellion and sin. Notice "sin" is singular, not plural. This is echoed in Luke 4:43 where Jesus stated his purpose:

> *I must also preach the kingdom of God to the other cities, because I was sent for this purpose.*

Notice that Jesus did not preach a religion in any capacity. Rather, Jesus came to preach a government, a nation, a country, namely the Kingdom of God—the King's dominion, authority, power, rule and influence on the earth.

Earlier in Luke 4, the enemy took Jesus up to a high place to tempt him. And he showed Jesus...um, all the *religions* of the world? No. He showed Jesus all the *kingdoms* of the world. Satan said they were given to him and that he could do whatever he wanted to do with them. In this case, he wanted to give them to Jesus...for a price:

> *And he led Him up and showed Him all the kingdoms of the world in a moment of time. And the devil said to Him, "I will give You all this domain and its glory, for it has been handed over to me, and I give it to whomever I want. Therefore if You worship before me, it shall all be Yours."*
>
> *Jesus replied to him, "It is written: 'You shall worship the Lord your God and serve Him only.'"*

Luke 4:5-8

Satan's offer to Jesus was simple: "Worship me and I'll give you all the kingdoms of the world."

Jesus' retort, however, left no confusion: "Nope. I'm going to get those kingdoms another way—the FATHER'S WAY!"

With that absolute rejection, the enemy lost his ability to negotiate with the last Adam, and Jesus' course was set. As it says in 1 John 3:8, Jesus' ministry was underway "to destroy the works of the devil."

Now let's look closer at John 3:16, although without our Western culture bias. Remember, when we look at scripture as God intended, we are studying: Who said it? Who did they say it to? What did it mean in that culture? How do I apply it in my life? To truly understand God's intent, we must read his word in context.

The verse starts prominently with: "For God...." I want you to feel this build up. "For God...so loved the world...." This word *loved* is where we get *agape*. We could say: "For God so *agaped* the world, that He gave His only Son, so that everyone who believes in Him will not perish, but have eternal life."

Sounds great, eh? Just like Sunday night revival service. "Cue the organ. Clear the rail. Gather contact info."

Now, that's the traditional response to this scripture. Instant salvation. But is that God's intent? When we look deeper, we gain a whole new light on what Jesus was saying. Notice what God loved. "For God so loved...the *world*."

The Greek meaning for *world* has absolutely nothing to do with humanity. Zero. Nada. Wala. The Greek word is *kosmos*. Now, it does not mean the outer space. (Sorry Carl Sagan.) The word *kosmos* means "order, government, governmental structure, to rule or what's being ruled, an order set up for governmental rule."

Of course, I'm not saying Jesus does not love humanity. Clearly, he does. But we need to understand what he was saying in this passage. He was saying: "God so loved the world...the *kosmos* order...that he gave his only begotten son."

This word *gave* is the Greek word *bido*, and it means "to command, allow, bestow or produce." The context is "to produce something." And what did God produce? He produced Jesus. This is what is meant by "he *gave* his only begotten son."

So, God loves order. We know that He does, right? The Bible says that we shouldn't even do things that are out of order. God is a God of order, a God of government. Everything he sets in order is done not just to look pretty, not just to sit on the shelf somewhere, but to function with purpose.

Because of his love for order—the world, government, structure— God sent his son to bring order to disorder. When Satan made the transaction in the garden, a new glory appeared, a nefarious glory, the weight of something ruling a situation. Through this weight came disorder. God sent his son Jesus into disorder to redeem order, to bring things back into order, back into his governmental structure. And whoever believes on Jesus—his purpose, calling or assignment—will not perish; they will not die. That word *die* means: "needs to be judged." So believers in Jesus will not have judgment released upon them but will live eternally.

Now traditional religion says, "Well, to live eternally, you just have to give Jesus your life. You've got to confess all of your sins. Your name needs to be written in the Lamb's Book of Life."

Let me tell you something. From what I've read and studied, everybody's name is in the Lamb's Book of Life. But if you don't get born again, it gets scratched out. Now, I hear the objections: "Doesn't God love everybody? Isn't everybody going to be born again?"

Jesus desires that none should perish (ref. 2 Peter 3:9) but no, everybody is not going to be born again.

Now, there's a system to shifting into the kingdom. When we look at John 3:16 through a kingdom perspective, we understand Jesus to say that God loved his governmental structure and that it had been filled with disorder.

The word *world* is different than the word *earth*. As Psalms 24:1 says:

> The earth is the Lord's, and all it contains,
> The world, and those who live in it.

God never lost the earth. He never lost ownership of the big blue marble he created back in Genesis 1. Instead, he lost the structure, the system, the governmental order that was functioning on the earth. It was corrupted; it was perverted by the enemy. Jesus came into the earth to take back the kingdom.

Consider:

> For the Son of Man has come to seek and to save that which
> was lost.

> Luke 19:10

The Bible says that Jesus came to seek and save "*that which* was lost." It does not say he came to seek and save "*those who* were lost." Yet we preach it that way. We've had some awesome altar calls that way. The truth is, Jesus came to seek and save *that which was lost*. People are not a *that*; they're a *those*. And in some cases, a *them*.

With this understanding, we have to ask: What was lost? The Kingdom of God was lost. It wasn't a religion that was lost. Adam didn't lose a hymn book or forget to go to Sunday School. It was a kingdom that was lost. God so loved his structure, his order, his government— that which had been hijacked by the enemy—that he sent his Son into the disorder to redeem it, to bring about order. And if there's anyone willing to believe in Jesus' assignment, purpose and calling, they can shift citizenship out of the kingdom of darkness and into the kingdom of light, and they will live eternally.

Here's an example of what I'm describing. My wife, Joan (pronounced Jo-ann), is a naturalized citizen. She was born Filipino. After she married me, she eventually became an American citizen. After all the paperwork, the money, legal mumbo-jumbo, she got it. Yeah! She didn't swim the Rio Grande. She flew across the Pacific and came in through Los Angeles. But when she traded that green card for a blue passport, she was no longer a visitor. She is now naturalized as a citizen of the United States of America. As such, she is now able to do everything any other citizen in America can do. Anything except be President. She can vote. She can run for office. She actually ran for the Statehouse in Hawaii twice.

So, when we look at John 3:16 through the lens of kingdom instead of religion, we see that Jesus stepped out of the unseen realm and into the seen realm, into disorder to bring it to order.

How did he do that? Through his death, burial, resurrection, ascension and sitting down at the right hand of the Father. He brought order. What did Jesus say in Matthew 28:18?

All authority in heaven and on earth has been given to Me.

In this scripture, the word *authority* is the Greek word *exousia*, which can be translated as "governmental authority." Jesus was saying that he stepped into the disorder, brought order and offered people an opportunity to switch citizenship from the kingdom of darkness to the kingdom of light. Not out of one religion into another religion, but out of one kingdom into another kingdom.

John the Baptist preached: "The Kingdom of God is at hand." He didn't preach "the modified Jewish religion is at hand." He was proclaiming that the government of God is at hand.

After his baptism, Jesus' entire message was: "The Kingdom of God; the government of God; the government of heaven is at hand. Repent! Change the way you think. Change the way you relate to God. The old way is not going to work. This is a new way.

Jesus brought the Kingdom of God to the earth. He stepped into the disorder and brought order. And he promised that whoever believes in him—his plan, purpose, assignment, and calling—will not perish but have everlasting life. They will live eternally.

We find this promise in Jesus' continued words in John 3:17-18:

For God did not send the Son into the world to judge the world, but so that the world might be saved through Him. The one who believes in Him is not judged; the one who does not believe has been judged already, because he has not believed in the name of the only Son of God.

Reading this through our kingdom lens, we understand that God did not send his Son into the disorder (the structure, the system) to judge the disordered system, but that the system, the government, the structure might be saved through him. Are you with me?

Remember: Who said it? Who is he talking to? What did it mean in their culture?

We cannot interpret scripture through our Western mindset and understand God's intent. It perverts everything. It brings us into religion, not into what Jesus came to do. Again, Jesus' purpose was to preach the Kingdom of God "that the world might be saved through him." The word *saved* in verse 17 is the Greek word *sozo*. It means "to make well, to cure, to ensure, to get well, to preserve, to recover and to restore."

In our ignorance, we have applied this message to our lives as religion, as in "we are getting saved." Yet that's not how Jesus applied it. He applied it to the kingdom—getting the Kingdom of God back and getting us back into the Kingdom. Why? To expand the Kingdom of God on the earth. He needs us to do that. That's his plan. It's been his plan all along. As Jesus tells us in Luke 12:32:

> Do not fear, little flock, for it is your Father's good pleasure to give you the kingdom.

Isn't that amazing? Jesus did not say God is excited about giving us a new, redefined, modified, souped-up religion. Not at all! He's giving us the kingdom—the world, the system, so that the *kosmos* may be saved through him.

From John 3:18:

> The one who believes in Him is not judged; the one who does not believe has been judged already, because he has not believed in the name of the only Son of God.

So the present kingdom is under judgment—the judgment of God. As harsh as this sounds, however, judgment really is good. Have you ever been to court? When the judge releases a judgment on your behalf, it's a good thing, isn't it? Yet we in Christianity have been taught that the judgment of God is a horrible thing. *He's coming to wipe everybody out. Hellfire, brimstones, fire falling from heaven, dogs and cats living together, mass hysteria. Jesus is returning and man is he ticked!* I hear it preached in many denominational churches including the one I was raised in. Yet the truth is that judgment, when it is in your favor, is an awesome thing.

Thank God! Jesus came and judged the system, the order, the *kosmos*.

> He who believes in Jesus is not judged. He who does not believe has been judged already because he has not believed in the name of the only begotten Son of God.

Now, when we talk about believing in the name of the Son of God, we're not just talking about the "name" Jesus. Religion has us tagging the name of Jesus at the end of our prayers like it's a lucky rabbit's foot or a four-leaf clover. It'll get us through a hard time. It's God's Platinum Visa card with no limit. We think the more we say "in Jesus' name," the sooner a miracle will fall from the sky. But it's simpler than that.

In "believe in the name," the word *name* in the Greek is *onoema*. It means "the cause, the authority of."

Religion has taught us to just believe in Jesus and you will be saved, with "saved" meaning he's going to get you out of here. You're going to miss hell and spend eternity in heaven...if you just believe in Jesus. The problem with this is that we start believing in that physical-bodied man Jesus, but that's not what he's talking about when he says by "believed in the name." Jesus is referring to his cause, his purpose.

To be clear (and to keep folks from showing up at my front door, my back door, and my bathroom window trying to gang-save me) I believe in the man Christ Jesus. I believe in him. I am born again through what he did. Hopefully so are you, my readers. But that belief is not just me putting my faith in this person called "Jesus." Rather, it's believing in what he embodies—his assignment and purpose on the earth—what he initiated while he was here. Not just that he was here in flesh and bone, but what the flesh and bone and spirit *did* while it was on the earth. That translates to name and authority. So, whoever believes in Jesus' name, authority or cause of the only begotten Son is released from judgment.

In verse 19.

And this is the judgment, that the Light has come into the world, and people loved the darkness rather than the Light; for their deeds were evil.

"That the light has come into the world"—the *kosmos*, meaning "structure, system, governmental structure." He is not speaking of multiple religions. He is speaking of two kingdoms—the kingdom of darkness and the kingdom of light. The *kosmos* (structure, order, governmental structure) was filled with darkness because the Prince of Darkness was ruling the world. He was in charge of the world since

Adam gave it away. That's the bad news. The good news is Jesus came to take it back! Hallelujah!

Verses 19-21:

And this is the judgment, that the Light [capital L, meaning Christ] has come into the world [the kosmos] and men loved the darkness [the kingdom of darkness] rather than the light, for their deeds were evil. For everyone who does evil hates the Light, and does not come to the Light, so that his deeds will not be exposed.

But the one who practices the truth comes to the Light, so that his deeds will be revealed as having been performed in God.

This is a powerful passage. Here's the judgment: light steps into the kingdom of darkness, redeems the order, redeems the structure, redeems the *kosmos* because of the Light, and then Jesus says "Here, I give it back to you—mankind. Go and do what Father God originally intended for you to do with it."

Amazing.

Now when we talk about light, the word *light* means "knowledge." Not lightbulb or illumination, but knowledge. The word *darkness* means "ignorance." It does not mean that there is no light in the room, that I can't see my hand in front of my face, but ignorance. Paul said:

Now concerning spiritual gifts, brethren, I would not have you ignorant.

1 Corinthians 12:1 KJV

He was not using the word *stupid.* That's a different concept. The great philosopher Forrest Gump said, "Stupid is as stupid does." Often, those two words are correlated in Western culture, but they're really two different meanings.

Ignorance means: "You don't know, but you could know." How do you find out what you don't know? You come into the Light. Religion is not "the Light." Jesus did not come to make us feel good or fierce or spiritual. He came to restore us back to God's original intent. We do that by coming out from under the kingdom of darkness and stepping into the kingdom of light—the Kingdom of God who is the Father of lights.

> *Every good thing given and every perfect gift is from above,*
> *coming down from the Father of lights, with whom there is*
> *no variation or shifting shadow.*

> James 1:17

Every good and perfect gift comes down from the Father of lights, gifts like knowledge and understanding and the power of God that flows from these. We are not looking at spiritual experiences, but supernatural experiences. There's a difference. *Super* here is *Supra* in the Greek and it refers to something in the unseen realm that manifests in the seen realm. It takes place in the *supra*—the supranatural—then shows up in the natural. As the Son of God was sent to redeem disorder on earth, Jesus stepped out of the unseen realm and into the seen realm to restore order to the colony of the Kingdom of God on earth.

If you believe in his cause and his purpose, then you can switch kingdoms. It's not about switching denominations or churches or religions. It's about switching kingdoms, allegiance, citizenship with all the rights, privileges and responsibilities as every other citizen.

Jesus didn't come to fix a broken religion. Neither did he come to give us a new religion. He came to restore order to the *kosmos*. God loves order. Look outside tonight when all the stars are in the sky and see how everything is fit in place and flowing together. All that is, moves according to his word. That's amazing. And it's all governmental. God governs those things by His word.

> *The heavens tell of the glory of God;*
> *And their expanse declares the work of His hands.*

> Psalm 19:1

Many won't come to the light because they're afraid they'll be found out. They love darkness more than they love light. These are they who will not be born again. But those who love truth come to the light so their deeds will be exposed, that their deeds may be manifested as having been wrought in God. These become born again into a new kingdom—the Kingdom of Light.

Whenever we come to God, God exposes all that is in us—usually privately—so we are able to repent from the kingdom of darkness and come to his kingdom. Yes, we change our citizenship instantly, but changing our ways takes a bit longer. Because we love truth, however, the light will manifest our deeds in us and through us.

This concept challenges religious mindsets. It's like when Jacob wrestled with God:

> *Then Jacob was left alone, and a man wrestled with him until daybreak. When the man saw that he had not prevailed against him, he touched the socket of Jacob's hip; and the socket of Jacob's hip was dislocated while he wrestled with him. Then he said, "Let me go, for the dawn is breaking."*
>
> *But he said, "I will not let you go unless you bless me."*
>
> *So he said to him, "What is your name?"*
>
> *And he said, "Jacob."*
>
> *Then he said, "Your name shall no longer be Jacob, but Israel; for you have contended with God and with men, and have prevailed."*

Genesis 32:24-28

Now, the Hebrew word translated "bless", as in "unless you bless me," can be better understood as "until you congratulate me."

Seems absurd, doesn't it? I can imagine God's reaction:

"Wait a minute, Jacob. I'm winning this thing. I just touched your thigh. You got a limp for life."

Why would God congratulate him? And yet God wanted to. He counted Jacob the winner even though Jacob wasn't the winner of the particular contest. God congratulated him so his purpose could be fulfilled through Jacob's life.

This parallels what Jesus did. God steps into a place. He wins the contest, and then he congratulates us on a job well done. Why? Because it gives us back our identity and purpose, and it enables us to go through life understanding that the poor in spirit will possess the Kingdom of God. From Jesus' sermon on the mount:

Blessed are the poor in spirit, for theirs is the kingdom of heaven.

Matthew 5:3

Ever wonder why Jesus lauded those who are poor in spirit? The answer lies within the definition. What does it mean to be poor in spirit? That we have holes in our spiritual pockets? That we are somehow spiritually bankrupt? Poor in spirit means "those who understand that they can do nothing without God." This is the awareness that Jesus blesses. Jesus authors everything and yet he shares the credit with us. He allows us to reap the reward. But all the time, we know it's him; it belongs to him; it's for him.

Of course, we have a part. Whatever God does on earth, he does through us—his people. He conceives the ideas, plants them in us, and expects our participation. The quality of such depends on our relationship with Christ. This is why we are called to maturity. As we grow, the will and heart of God flow through us and merge with us with greater purity. When our hearts come into sync with his heart, our will becomes his will. No, God doesn't do everything. Rather, he leads and supplies everything. We, the body, have a vital role, but he is the head. Together, we are all expressions of God's presence on earth.

For by Him all things were created, both in the heavens and on earth, visible and invisible, whether thrones or dominions or rulers or authorities- all things have been created through Him and for Him.

Colossians 1:16

We're debunking the spirit of religion, replacing it with the knowledge that God gave us a kingdom, one that he redeemed through his Son Jesus Christ.

6

Reign

LET US DISPLACE THE SPIRIT OF RELIGION that has held us in bondage for centuries. Jesus did not give us a religion. He came to redeem the Kingdom of God on earth. Let's explore this truth through scriptures. First up, Acts 1.

> *The first account I composed, Theophilus, about all that Jesus began to do and teach, until the day when He was taken up* to heaven, *after He had given orders by the Holy Spirit to the apostles whom He had chosen. To these He also presented Himself alive after His suffering, by many convincing proofs, appearing to them over* a period of *forty days and speaking of things regarding the Kingdom of God.*

> Acts 1:1-3

Notice the keyword *began*, as in "all that Jesus *began* to do and teach...." Folks, Jesus was just getting started. He did not just hop out of the grave and float off to Heaven. Instead, he walked around for 40 days with his disciples and some others who also rose with him. Abraham's bosom was emptied of souls by the King of Kings. He spent his last days on earth before ascending "Speaking of things regarding the Kingdom of God." Not things regarding religion, not even the Jewish religion, but the Kingdom of God. Even after his resurrection, Jesus was teaching the Kingdom. Indeed, nowhere in the Book of Acts do we find Jesus or the apostles talking about religion, not even the Apostle Paul:

> *When they had set a day for Paul, people came to him at his lodging in large numbers; and he was explaining to them by solemnly testifying about the kingdom of God and trying to*

persuade them concerning Jesus, from both the Law of Moses and from the Prophets, from morning until evening.

Acts 28:23

Paul was persuading people concerning the Kingdom of God, not religion. He obviously felt strongly about not following religion. In fact, he confronted Peter for behaving religiously when gentile believers were present.

But when Cephas came to Antioch, I opposed him to his face, because he stood condemned. For prior to the coming of some men from James, he used to eat with the Gentiles; but when they came, he began to withdraw and separate himself, fearing those from the circumcision. The rest of the Jews joined him in hypocrisy, with the result that even Barnabas was carried away by their hypocrisy. But when I saw that they were not straightforward about the truth of the gospel, I said to Cephas in the presence of all, "If you, being a Jew, live like the Gentiles and not like the Jews, how is it that you compel the Gentiles to live like Jews?

Galatians 2:11-14

Peter's approach was based on religion: "We cannot even hang out with those folks. They have not been circumcised." He got in trouble for that. Can you imagine Peter getting into trouble? (I can't imagine Peter *not* getting into trouble.) Paul knew that the gospel was about the Government of God, not the religion of God.

Preaching the kingdom of God and teaching things concerning the Lord Jesus Christ with all openness, unhindered.

Acts 28:31

This is how Paul spent his last days, teaching the Kingdom of God and the Lord Jesus Christ, not the religion of such. When we are teaching kingdom, we are teaching Jesus.

About 20 years ago when I began to discover this teaching, it wrecked me. I'd pray: "God, why are You dealing with me about these things?"

Over the years, the Lord has answered me, saying: "Because I cannot do on the earth what I want to do. My intent, the intent of my heart, cannot be realized through a system of darkness."

God is not going to establish his kingdom on earth through religion. It's just not going to happen. Indeed, it cannot.

And as if that wasn't enough wrecking for one lifetime, he has also said to me: "Greg, I am not obligated to answer anybody's prayers that do not line up with my purpose."

Sounds like God means business.

He also showed me how frustrated the church is because we are not seeing our prayers answered. We are not seeing the things come to pass that we are asking God to do. We are not seeing cities change. We are not seeing our nation change the way we are believing God to change it. Why? Because we have been trying to see these things manifested through a religious system, a religious *kosmos*, and not the Kingdom *kosmos*.

When I was 17, I received the baptism of Holy Spirit, and the Lord said to me: "Greg, you are going to have to unlearn almost as much as you have learned."

I thought, *Unlearn? How dare you, God! Lord, how can you say that to me? Don't you know who I am? I am a third-generation minister!"*

For God's information (and yours, lol), my grandfather was a Baptist minister for 75 years. He helped start the first African American Bible College in Mississippi. It was in Mount Bayou, Mississippi. He was doing things nobody else was doing. He taught me almost everything that I know. Why would I have to unlearn all that he taught me?

Then God showed me that most of the time when people hear "unlearn," they feel it will dishonor those who taught them. I revere my grandfather, and I intend to honor the legacy he left me. That's when the Lord said: "You are not dishonoring him. You are honoring him by building on what he taught you."

That made sense. So many times, we get hung up on where we were raised and what we have been doing and forget about where God is taking us next.

I have heard people say, "I will be Pentecostal all my life. My grandmama was Pentecostal. My great-grandmama was Pentecostal. We are going to stay Pentecostal 'till Jesus comes, bless God."

Some people simply cannot leave a church denomination because they have been there forever, their families have been there forever, their history is there. They disembarked from the Mayflower with tags on their coats: *Pentecostal 1* and *Pentecostal 2*.

FAMILY BUSINESS

For all the good that religion has done—and there has been some—we have to get out of our religious structures. God will not do what he wants to do on the earth through a religious mindset that produces disorder. He will not do it. God does not adapt to us; we adapt to him. He does not work in the things that we give him; we work on what he gives us. Remember: the only opinion that matters is the King's.

Think of the book of Esther. How did Esther ever get favor with the King? By reaching the King's heart. And when she had favor with the King, she was able to get legislation enacted that protected the Jews. The King loved her, and so he would do anything for her. That is where we are with the Father. We need to get into his heart, not as the overarching controller of the universe, but as Abba...Daddy. God is our Abba and we are in the family business. Abba and Sons.

What is the family business? Our Daddy is not a cobbler. He is not a plumber or a banker or a lawyer. He is not even a carpenter or a doctor. Hey, he's not even a preacher. Our Daddy is a King, and his business is Kingdom. His business is not religion. His business is government. Therefore, you and I, when we are born again, are born again into government as part of Daddy's family. That is what he says in the Book of Matthew 16:18:

> *And I also say to you that you are Peter, and upon this rock I will build My church; and the gates of Hades will not overpower it.*

Remember: *church* is a governmental word; it is the ekklesia.

That word *build* means family, as in "I am going to build my church *from* my family. I am going to release a legislative authority, a governing arm on the earth."

The Kingdom of God is family, and every citizen is a son or a daughter. There are no second-class citizens in this country, no green cards, no illegal aliens. We are all naturalized citizens. We are all related to the King as children of his blood. As a matter of fact, the Bible says we are kings of the King. How? Because Jesus is King of kings and Lord of lords. That is not talking about kings in earthly government. It is about God's sons and daughters. We are a royal priesthood, just as Peter proclaimed:

> *But you are a chosen people, a royal priesthood, a holy nation, a people for God's own possession, so that you may proclaim the excellencies of Him who has called you out of darkness into His marvelous light.*

> 1 Peter 2:9

We are a royal priesthood not after the Levitical order, but after the Melchizedek order, because Jesus did not come through the Levitical order. Jesus was from the tribe of Judah. That is different from the tribe of Levi. Jesus did not come to adapt to what the Levites were doing. He came to bring a whole other order of a priesthood, one which operates from the power of an endless life. In a Levitical order, they needed new priests every so often because they kept dying. But not with Jesus. He is a Priest and a King forever; therefore, we are in the same royal priesthood after the order of Melchizedek:

You are My Son,
Today I have fathered You"
"You are a priest forever
According to the order of Melchizedek.

Hebrews 5:5-6

Was Melchizedek a religious man? No. He was a King. Neither are we of a religious order. Let us go to Romans 5:17:

For if by the transgression of the one, death reigned through the one, much more those who receive the abundance of grace and of the gift of righteousness will reign in life through the One, Jesus Christ.

"For if by the transgression of the one..."

Who is the one? Adam.

"Death reigned through the one..."

So, Adam transgressed. Because of his transgression, Adam surrendered the Kingdom to the enemy. He gave Satan the ability to be king. Okay, now follow me here.

This word *transgression* does not mean "sins" in the way you conduct yourself on a daily basis. This word *transgression* means "a false step or to trespass, to fall in or to fall away or fallen away." When we use the word *transgression* in the Greek, it is the word *parapipto* and it means that we have made a false step; we have become out of step with something.

Professional dancers have a flow about them. It is beautiful when they are both in step together. One false step and the whole thing is ruined. Somebody is going to break a leg and lose a tiara.

Well, this word *transgression* is a picture of humanity and God in a beautiful dance. They are in the rhythm of the music; they are in the flow. God is leading. We are flowing and dancing with him. Yet if we get out of step, we break up the whole dance. That is *transgression*. One false step causes you to get out of rhythm and the whole thing tumbles to the ground.

I realize this definition does not agree with what we've been taught. This is not "sin" as "missed the mark or rebelled," but it literally describes Adam. When he surrendered, he got out of the rhythm of heaven. He got out of step. He transgressed against God and he gave death the power to reign.

We know that *death* in the Greek is *thanatos* and it speaks of evil, like a pestilence working in your life. That is the devil. "Death reigned through the one." Note, however, that death reigned and functioned through Adam, not the devil. Whoever said the devil was strong enough to reign? He has his scepter and his crown tilted on the side of his head. He must be reeling from the thoughts of hell. The devil is not looking forward to hell. He does not rule from Hell. Yes, the poem *Paradise Lost* quotes the devil as saying: "Better to rule in hell than serve in heaven," but that is fiction, not scripture. (Great poet, that Milton, but a terrible theologian.)

Make no mistake: Jesus owns hell. Death, hell and the grave are in the King's domain. Remember the transitions. We went from the Kingdom of Light to the Kingdom of Darkness; from the Kingdom of Life to the Kingdom of Death. It all worked through Adam. The man did not change; it was the kingdom that changed. Adam was in the Kingdom of Life until he transgressed, then the Kingdom of Death was working.

Therefore, just as through one man sin entered into the world, and death through sin, and so death spread to all mankind, because all sinned...

Romans 5:12

The good news, however, is that this is not the end of the story.

For if by the offense of the one, death reigned through the one, much more will those who receive the abundance of grace and of the gift of righteousness reign in life through the One, Jesus Christ.

Romans 5:17

We who receive the abundance of grace and the gift of righteousness will reign. Not just recover. Not just scrape by. But reign. Well, reign where? Reign in life. When? Today. In the here and now. Not in the sweet by and by. Not in heaven way out yonder somewhere. Not after a premillennial snatching up rapture and a thousand-year millennial rule and all of the yada yada yadas of Western eschatology. Not after a return of Jesus. Not after a catching away of the church. Not after a tribulation. Not after the judgment of the devil. None of that.

We reign in life, this life, where you and I are today. Life is now!

We are not waiting on Jesus; he is waiting on us. We are not hanging out on earth practicing rapture. "OK, everybody. When I say 'three,' jump into the air as high as you can. Ready? One, two...." Stupid.

We are already risen with Christ.

Therefore, if you have been raised with Christ, keep seeking the things that are above, where Christ is, seated at the right hand of God.

Colossians 3:1

We are already with Christ in heavenly places.

But God, being rich in mercy, because of His great love with which He loved us, even when we were dead in our wrongdoings, made us alive together with Christ (by grace you have been saved), and raised us up with Him, <u>and seated us with Him in the heavenly places in Christ Jesus,</u> so that in the ages to come He might show the boundless riches of His grace in kindness toward us in Christ Jesus.

Ephesians 2:4-7

Jesus' whole purpose in coming to earth was to empower us to occupy colony earth. Recall his words just before he left terra firma:

And Jesus came up and spoke to them, saying, "All authority in heaven and on earth has been given to Me. Go, therefore, and make disciples of all the nations, baptizing them in the name of the Father and the Son and the Holy Spirit, teaching them to follow all that I commanded you; and behold, I am with you always, to the end of the age."

Matthew 28:18-20

In essence, Jesus was saying: "All power and authority has been given to me in heaven and earth. Now you go and rule, go into every *kosmos*, every system, every structure and establish my government. Be my governmental representation as ambassador sons and daughters, and shift the entirety of this world into my Kingdom."

Glory to God! Here is the key: Those who receive the abundance of grace and the gift of righteousness will reign in life through the One, Jesus Christ. Death reigned through one Adam. Kingdom reigns through One Jesus Christ.

It is Jesus who gives us the ability to reign. This word *reign* is a powerful word. It is the word *basileuo* in the Greek. *Basileuo* comes through the root *basileia* which means "to be king, become king and to reign." It refers to one who is reigning. That's present tense, not past or future tense. It means that those who receive the abundance of grace and the gift of righteousness will be kings in life. You, I, anyone in Christ, will reign in this life through the One, Jesus Christ.

The purpose of Jesus was not to make us religious people and to get us into heaven. His purpose was to make us kings to rule on the earth.

So, what does this reign look like? Are we ruling over everybody? Do we have all the authority? No, we are not reigning in the conventional sense. This is not a web of tyrants and tridents, despots and demigods, thrones and overthrown. That's the world's idea of reigning, and it's a mess. God's reigning is different.

ONE BODY

In Genesis, God called mankind to rule over the fish in the sea, the birds of the air, over everything that walked, crawled or slithered in the dirt. In short, man was to reign over everything that God created ...

except for mankind. God never intended for you and me to rule over one another. We were intended to rule together on the earth on his behalf. That is why we are referred to as his body, members in particular (see 1 Corinthians 12:25-27), where we function and flow as one unit.

One of the things I have learned about Jewish culture historically, is that it is more about community than the individual. That is how the Jewish people conduct themselves. Their lives are not just about their individual existence. Their lives are intertwined with the community's life.

There's the story told in Joshua 7 of an unfortunate man named Achan who hid forbidden treasure in his tent. Israel had just lost a battle in which 36 men were killed. Seeking answers, Joshua fell on his face and cried before the Lord. The Lord's reply left no question where things stood:

Stand up! Why is it that you have fallen on your face? Israel has sinned, and they have also violated My covenant which I commanded them. And they have even taken some of the things designated for destruction, and have both stolen and kept it a secret. Furthermore, they have also put them among their own things.

So in the morning you shall come forward by your tribes. And it shall be that the tribe which the Lord selects by lot shall come forward by families, and the family which the Lord selects shall come forward by households, and the household which the Lord selects shall come forward man by man. And it shall be that the one who is selected with the things designated for destruction shall be burned with fire, he and all that belongs to him, because he has violated the covenant of the Lord, and because he has committed a disgraceful thing in Israel.'"

Joshua 7:10-11, 14-15

Notice: even though God used the pronoun *they*, it was "the one" who was disobedient that caused all the problems. This is similar to

Romans 5:12: "Therefore, just as through one man sin entered into the world, and death through sin, and so death spread to all mankind." In this case, the entire nation of Israel suffered for Achan's sin. This is how it was among the Jews. Indeed, it had to be. They lived and died as a nation. Things did not turn out well for Achan, but the nation survived.

Western Culture has made Christianity about each of us, but it is not about the individual. It is about you and I and them and us as members of Jesus' Body—as members of his ekklesia—the legislative arm of heaven that he has called us to be.

The ultimate goal of the family that God restored through the death, burial and resurrection of Jesus was not to give us an individual relationship with Jesus per se, but for us to have a corporate relationship with God the Father. As individual members of this body, we do what each of us is designed to do. Together, we cause the kingdoms of this world to become the kingdoms of our God. We live and die as a body. There is no other way. If I have the strongest right arm in the history of right arms, but there is cancer reigning in my pancreas, guess what? I'm not going to live long unless I get that taken care of, right arm or no right arm.

Unfortunately, we do not think like that in America. We are free folks, rugged individualists, entitled self-seekers. Now, there is nothing wrong with personal freedom, but the Kingdom of God is more. It is about all of us walking together with God. We rarely hear that message in America, but it is vital. No single one of us is going to win the world or their city or their community. To shift culture requires the ekklesia collectively coming together and being who God intended us to be.

It's not about getting people into our church buildings, but getting them into the Kingdom. God does not really give a donkey's hind end about our building, our steeple, our hundred-year-old pews. He cares about his church—the ekklesia—a kingdom people that are in a culture to change a culture and cause the kingdoms of this world to become the Kingdom of our God.

Now, scripture says there are two things we need in order to reign: an abundance of grace and righteousness. Of grace, we read:

For if by the offense of the one, death reigned through the one, much more will those who receive the abundance of grace and of the gift of righteousness reign in life through the One, Jesus Christ.

Romans 5:17

(We will discuss righteousness in the following chapter.)

In Western Christianity, grace is misunderstood as special liberty in life, tacit permission to do whatever we want to do. But that's not grace. It might be mercy or an excuse to evade judgment, but it is not grace. Grace is empowerment.

Romans 5:17 tell us that grace is actually a component of reigning as a king. We need grace in our lives to release us to be kings in the sphere of influence that God has given us. The word *grace* here in the Greek is *charis* and it means "blessing, concession, credit, favor, gratitude and thankfulness."

Now, in this same passage, four words before *grace*, is the word *receive*. This is a very important verb. It is the word *lambano* in the Greek. (Not "La Bamba," but *lambano*.) The word *lambano* means "to accept, caught." Scripture is saying that Jesus caught something for you and said, "Good catch." Indeed, Jesus received something and credited it to our account, saying "Now, live as a king. Not as a religious person trying to make it to heaven, but as a reigning person who knows what you are called to do."

Scripture says that those who receive (*lambano*) this grace, obtain an abundance of empowerment. So, how do we get grace? Well...we receive it.

Jesus assigns us territories to rule and reign in life, areas he wants us to steward. This might be material things like cars, buildings, or land. It might involve organizations such as businesses, churches or schools. It will certainly involve talents, skills and anointings. And it will likely be related to our ministerial gifts and callings. In essence, everything Jesus brings to our lives is a form of grace. And these become the means to do what he's called us to do. These things are God's empowerment to rule and reign.

In the process, we are called to steward our gifts wisely, not abusing them nor letting them corrupt us. Much of what Jesus calls us to do involves money—the cash to start business, launch ministries, conduct outreaches, or simply keep the lights on at home while we devote ourselves to intercessory prayer. We must never lose sight of the fact that our gifts are his gifts; our empowerment is his Spirit. He teaches us, leads us, corrects us and empowers us as we fulfill our part.

We receive these gifts from God's hand to our hands and draw them into our lives to use and grow, just as Adam was supposed to do in the garden. Eden was still God's Garden, but Adam was to steward it, rule it, *basilio* (operate as a king) in his metron.

God's grace is God's; it is his blessing and his concession. He concedes grace to us. We do not concede grace to him. It is to his credit, not our credit, that we succeed. He is saying, "I am gracious. I am giving you something that is mine. It is for my purposes." It is his favor, not our favor. More so, it is his gratitude and thankfulness. Religion tells us we need to be thankful for our salvation. However, if it was not for God's thankfulness—his grace towards us—we could not be thankful in the first place.

So, God was thankful for me. Does that make sense? God had gratitude towards me, towards you. See, religion says, "No, no. That is flipped. You got to flip it. You have got to have gratitude toward God." You do, but you have got to have thankfulness toward God. God did not have those things towards you, but actually grace is the expression of God's gratitude towards you, and His thankfulness toward you!

Religion says, "We are saved by grace. It is God's unmerited favor. I never did anything to earn it." While this sounds noble, it approaches life through a beat-down, defeated mindset. But as God's family, we are not to live by struggles and defeat. We are to live from the position of the victory of a risen Christ.

That is Kingdom. We *were* sinners—past tense. If there is any truth to the phrase "unmerited favor," it is God's ability to do in me that which I cannot do in myself. He offers grace to reign. We have to receive it; we have to pull it; we have to *lambano* it into our lives! When we do that, we receive an abundance of grace full of his gratitude, his thankfulness, his favor, his blessing and his concession.

It is nothing we could do on our own. As kings, we must be able to function as he intended us to function. Dance, flow and reign.

7

Coronation

WE HAVE BEEN STUDYING THE MARVELOUS GIFT OF RIGHTEOUSNESS from Romans 5:17. Righteousness is the second thing we need to reign, grace being the first (ref. chapter 6).

> *For if by the offense of the one, death reigned through the one, much more will those who receive the abundance of grace and of the gift of righteousness reign in life through the One, Jesus Christ.*

This word *gift* is the word *do* in the Greek and it means "without cost, without paying, freely, something bestowed upon you, to coronate."

To coronate? Yes, that is in the meaning. As in *reign.* Where do we reign? We reign "in life."

What a gift! God could have said: "Look, you dirty, rotten sinner, I am going to put up with you just to get you out of this old, damned earth and get you into heaven where you can live with me in a place where sin does not dwell. You just hang on; I will get you out one day. Just hang on; keep believing; keep submitting."

Thankfully, that was not his approach to us. Instead, he gave grace to us. He *"do" ("gift") us into* coronation. He made us sons and daughters of God. He made us kings!

This coronation was one of righteousness. *Righteousness* means: "I have a right relationship with God. I have right standing with God." Yet the depth of that is more than right standing; it is right relationship, which means God coronated us, gifted us relationship. He made us kings in right relationship with him. It was a gift. We did nothing to earn it.

Religion does not fit into this definition. It will not work here. Scripture is saying: "If you will receive the abundance of grace—the gift of righteousness—you will be a king in life." This kingship is not in name only; God does not bestow honorary titles. He gives us responsibility. When he makes us kings in this life, he places us in a sphere of influence—a *metron*.

Our responsibility is to carry the king's sovereign dominion into these places of influence, causing everyone in those places that we influence to become so hungry for what we carry that they want to trade their old passport in for a new one. They will not want to join a church; they will not want to join a religion; they will not be worried about ordinances, rules and regulations. They will only want to meet our King. Hallelujah!

The king in every nation has their own language. We need to change our language. We need to stop asking people to come to church. We need to start asking people to come meet our King. That is what He wants. He wants to get them into the Kingdom so they can find their purpose and identity and make their way back home as sons and daughters.

This wrecks almost everything we have been taught. Yet it is exactly what Jesus taught two millennium ago!

But seek ye first the Kingdom of God, and his righteousness;
and all these things shall be added unto you.

Matthew 6:33 KJV

The word *first* in the Greek is the word *pro*. It means "above all, first in priority, first in responsibility, first in importance."

The phrase "Kingdom of God" is the Greek word *Basilia*.

In the phrase "and His righteousness," the word *righteousness* here means "justice." What is the justice of God? Justice comes from the word *judge*. Jesus did not come to judge but to save.

For God did not send the Son into the world to judge the
world, but so that the world might be saved through Him.

John 3:17

His salvation is justice; to correct; innocence and righteousness.

The two components to reigning are: the abundance of grace and the gift of righteousness. The promise of Jesus is: "Seek first my Kingdom and my righteousness, and everything you need in life will be given to you." (See Matthew 6:33). *Everything* you need in life will be given to you.

Most of our days are spent trying to secure what we are going to eat and wear, where we are going to live, what we will drive, where our kids will play and go to school—the "necessities of life." Yet this scripture says to not focus on these things.

What will happen then? Will I be evicted? Are they going to repossess our house? Do I need to keep making my payments? What is going on? I need to work.

God provides those things.

You mean they are going to fall out of thin air?

Not at all. I tried that route one time. It did not work well. That was back in my hair days.

What does it mean, then?

It means we find our area, our sphere of influence, that God has called us to work in. And we work for him. We do not work for money or payments or to keep the wolf from the door. We work to honor the King of kings. We work as unto him. We work as if it is our calling...because that's exactly what it is. (See Colossians 3:23)

Consider this famous proverb:

Train up a child in the way he should go: and when he is old, he will not depart from it.

Proverbs 22:6 KJV

Now, look at this a little differently: "Train up a child in the way they are *bent* (or *inclined*) and when they are old, they will walk in it."

As ones created in God's image, we all have talents, inclinations, bendings—things we gravitate toward, things we are good at- callings.

Whatever it is that God built us for, we find that place, we walk in that place as a grace—an empowerment—for us to operate there. There is a release of influence for us there. As we begin to walk in that place that God created for us to be, to function and flow in, we will begin to see great favor released in our lives. That favor that God releases to us will enable others to want to know King Jesus.

> *For even the Son of Man did not come to be served, but to serve, and to give His life as a ransom for many.*
>
> Mark 10:45

We are not talking about soul winning; we are talking about redeeming the kidnapped. Jesus came to give his life as a ransom. That means to "pay the price" for those held captive, those held in the Kingdom of darkness, those wanting to come to the Kingdom of Light. This requires a significant change in our thinking. We are not trying to get people into a religion. We are trying to get them into the Kingdom where they find who God created them to be as his sons and daughters; where they are able to go out themselves and cause the kingdoms of this world to become the kingdoms of our God. This is how kingdom grows.

Whether we are a business person, a bus driver, a doctor, a minister, a butcher, a baker or a candlestick maker, we are all part of the ekklesia. As such, God has given us the ability to *Basilio* in that place—to change the culture of that place to look like Heaven.

OUR PATTERN

We need to understand that when Satan showed Jesus the kingdoms of the world and offered them to him, he knew who Jesus was. Recall that at Jesus' baptism, the Father showed up and announced to the world: "This is my beloved Son in whom I am well pleased" (Matthew 3:17). God identified him on the earth at that particular point. If nothing else, this certainly alerted the enemy that the Messiah was here, and that is why he swooped in and tried to tempt him away from the Father's plan.

In Isaiah, God told how the Messiah would come, that he would be birthed:

> *For a Child will be born to us, a Son will be given to us;*
> *And the government will rest on His shoulders;*
> *And His name will be called Wonderful Counselor,*
> *Mighty God, Eternal Father, Prince of Peace.*

> Isaiah 9:6

Satan knew all this, and that's why he tried to tempt Jesus in this way. He would not have offered the kingdoms of this world to just anybody.

We know that Jesus prevailed in this temptation from his title: Lord of Lords. He did it as man! Praise the Lord!

The word *lord* comes from the word *Adonai* meaning "owner." The Lord owns everything. Jesus is Lord (big L). We are lords (little l). In that capacity, we are the ones that steward the King's land and finances. The "big L" Lord has possession of all the finances in the land. We know the earth is the Lord's from Psalms:

> *The earth is the Lord's, and all it contains,*
> *The world, and those who live in it.*

> Psalm 24:1

We get the term *Lord* in our modern-day usage of *landlord*: "those who own that piece of land and we rent from them." But in this particular capacity, we are in charge of the Father's land, the earth, and we are in charge of his finances—all that he has in his kingdom here. Which is why nations will be judged.

JUDGEMENT

We know from scripture that in the end, there will be judgement of sheep nations and goat nations:

> "But when the Son of Man comes in His glory, and all the angels with Him, then He will sit on His glorious throne. And all the nations will be gathered before Him; and He will

separate them from one another, just as the shepherd
separates the sheep from the goats; and He will put the sheep
on His right, but the goats on the left.

Matthew 25:31-33

Of course, God wants all nations to be sheep nations. That's why he tells us to cause the kingdoms of this world (*kosmos*) to become the kingdoms of our God.

Go, therefore, and make disciples of all the nations, baptizing
them in the name of the Father and the Son and the Holy
Spirit, teaching them to follow all that I commanded you; and
behold, I am with you always, to the end of the age."

Matthew 28:19-20

By nations, he means both ethnic groups and governmental nations. God loves nations.

Now, none of this is predetermined. We have the ability to shift nations, but we have to use it. The Bible does say that nations can be saved in a single day (ref. Isaiah 66). I believe it will happen, though not through a religious system of preaching "get out of hell free, fire insurance," lol. No, the King is here and he wants these kingdoms to submit to his kingdom, and then he will bless them.

Blessed is the nation whose God is the Lord,
The people whom He has chosen for His own inheritance

Psalm 33:12

BLESSING

Now, blessing is different from a command. A command would be something spoken to you to go do. The context of Genesis 1, however, is what God spoke into us for us to become." When God said...

Be fruitful and multiply, and fill the earth, and subdue it; and
rule over the fish of the sea and over the birds of the sky and
over every living thing that moves on the earth

Genesis 1:28

...it was not a command to go and do. Rather, he spoke it *into us.* It became part of our make-up, our DNA as mankind. As we move throughout the earth, that word is manifested. As we live our lives, we are blessed; we are multiplying, subduing, ruling, kingdom-ing. That is the blessing. He built it in us. So, as we be who we are, we become who he designed us to be. Doing his will is ingrained in our nature. That is why people who defy or deny God are never fulfilled. They set up a war within themselves that quickly becomes self-defeating. Man's place of operation is the presence of God.

RIGHTEOUSNESS

As discussed earlier, the word *eden* means "presence." The garden was not necessarily a geographical location. Rather, the original man and woman operated out of the presence of God, the place God put them on the earth. Yes, it was a piece of geography, but what made it special was the place where God's presence dwelled, thus enabling man to be who God created them to be.

As redeemed men and women, the gift of righteousness is our coronation. We have been given the title "king." He is the King of kings. When we rule in that authority, we are the "little k" kings. The gift of righteousness changes everything.

Consider the fact that there cannot be two kings in one country. Now, we know Jesus is King. If we were in heaven, however, we would not be kings any longer. God created a colony called earth, a place into which he wanted to extend his influence, will, intent and purpose. He put us here. Therefore, we can be kings in this outpost of what God has in his heart, which is the establishment of his Kingdom.

A good example is the king of Portugal. The king of Portugal colonized Brazil. In the colonizing of Brazil, he wanted his son to be a king. He knew, however, that he had to die or descend the throne for his son to be king. As long as his son was with him, the son would always be a prince. So, he set his son up in Brazil as king. The son could be a king in another land, in another territory, but he could not be a king if he ever returned to Portugal. He would always be a prince in Portugal.

Jesus is the King of kings. The King of Glory! We are kings because we are in a territory that is not heaven. We are here as kings on the earth to expand his will and heart here in colony earth.

THE ARMY

Every Kingdom has an army. There is an army to the Kingdom of God. It consists of the angels of God—the angelic host—and ourselves. Now, when I hear people say: "We are the army of God," I reply: "No we are not, at least, not entirely. The angels are the army of God. We lead the army. We are kings."

Our place on the battlefield is not as soldiers. We are not of military rank. We are not privates, lieutenants, colonels or generals. Can you imagine the enemy seeing a thousand kings arrayed against him instead of a thousand privates with a few lieutenants, captains and a general? We are kings, which is higher than generals. Kings deploy armies. We lead and direct angelic armies.

When we go into battle, we fight as kings. Kings carry authority. They war with declarations, decrees, worship and prayer. Angels war with deeds. They get done what we declare.

Jehoshaphat is a great example of this. As King, he consulted with the Prophet Elisha to defeat the Moabites. They called the worshippers so that Elisha could hear from the Lord. Elisha then told Jehoshaphat what to do, and he instructed the army to do it.

We must come into the right order to release the angelic host to carry out their part of the battle. We need to see ourselves as Father sees us. We need that identity in the depths of our being so when we face situations, we will act and operate as he created us to be, not what religion taught or bad theology has conditioned us to think.

So, one army, two areas of responsibility—our authority and angels' deeds. The weapons of our warfare.

JEALOUSY

Often, our greatest contributors to the Kingdom of God are folks who come from outside our Western civilization of religion. This is one reason we are told to bless Israel in the New Covenant context.

> *And I will bless those who bless you [Israel],*
> *And the one who curses you I will curse.*
> *And in you all the families of the earth will be blessed.*

> Genesis 12:3

Israel should be in our top priority of blessings. We give them favor. We love them. We support them. We do not curse them. We do not do anything that would harm them. We back them and stand with them.

I love taking people into Israel. You get to see the Holy Land from a kingdom perspective. It is not a religious tour at all; it is a kingdom tour. You get to see from the kingdom perspective how Israel operates and how we are to partner with them, love them and make them a little jealous so they want to come to Jesus.

Our guide, who was a colonel (retired) in the Israeli Army said to us once as we were looking over the Golan Heights into Syria to where he had fought a battle. He told us a story of that battle, and then he told us that he did not believe Jesus was Messiah until he began meeting people who were born again. He began to cry at that point. He said how jealous he became because the Gentile loves his God more than he, a Jew, loved his God. It was not really the Jesus story that drew him as much as it was the love for God. It caused him to pay attention to what made the Gentiles love his God. It was the love of Jesus. The love that the Gentiles had for his God made him investigate who this Jesus was.

We must love Israel. We must pray for Israel. We must pray for the peace of Jerusalem. I believe that with all my heart. I believe that we are going to see an incredible harvest of Jewish people. And we need them. We cannot build kingdom without them.

8

The Message of Jesus

WE ARE MOVING OUT OF RELIGION AND INTO KINGDOM—glory to God! We have been set free from the religious Egypt and are journeying to the Promised Land of the Kingdom. This transformation has been the missing element for reformation and transformation. You see, God is not obligated to answer our prayers when we are praying outside his will for our lives. He will not transform cities and nations out of an old system he has not approved. God answers prayers out of his kingdom. Why? Because he gets glory. It all belongs to Him.

Jesus' purpose on the earth was to preach the Kingdom of God. Nowhere in the gospels do we find that Jesus preached any other message. He never preached the gospel of prosperity; never preached the gospel of deliverance; never preached the gospel of healing; never preached the gospel of salvation. Instead, he preached the gospel of the kingdom. And when he did, all of those other things—prosperity, deliverance, healing, salvation and more—manifested in the process.

In the beginning, God governed with his words, and so did man. When God blessed Adam and Eve in the Garden, he did so by speaking to them. With his words, he imparted grace—the power to accomplish the spoken mission. Key, however, is that God spoke blessings *into* the very nature of mankind. His blessing shaped the DNA of who Adam and Eve were and who future generations would be. Therefore, fulfilling the great commission to "be fruitful and multiply, fill the earth, subdue it and rule" wasn't something mankind simply aspired to do. It wasn't merely a bar that God set to see how high they could jump. Rather, it was a mandate they executed because it came from the core of their beings. It was who they were, just as it is who we are.

Why do we climb mountains? Because they're there!

Following God's lead, Adam named the animals, the herbs, the trees, all the things that God created. In naming everything, Adam invoked God's original intent for them through his words.

FIRST THINGS FIRST

After Adam fell, however, he had to govern with his hands. He tilled the ground to get the cursed earth to respond to him. He fought thorns and thistles for the herbs that sustained him. The earth no longer responded to his voice. It only responded to his calloused hands and fevered brow.

Then Jesus came along preaching kingdom to a population who only knew how to fight the soil:

> But seek first His kingdom and His righteousness, and all these things will be provided to you.

Matthew 6:33

This was more than remarkable. This was revolutionary. He was teaching that when we start making other things priority, nothing works. Everything flows from the Kingdom of God. Indeed, it did so for Adam until he changed his priorities. Jesus came to reverse that. "Your first priority is to seek the kingdom and His righteousness, and everything will be added unto you."

As stated in a previous chapter, the word *first* in this passage is the word *pro* in the Greek, meaning "first in importance, first in priority, first in order." That same word *pro* is also used in 1 Corinthians 12:28 where it says:

> And God has appointed these in the church: first apostles, second prophets, third teachers, after that miracles, then gifts of healings, helps, administrations, varieties of tongues.

Jesus was saying that to be in alignment with the word of God and the heart of God, our first priority is to be kingdom, not religion. Jesus did not come to give us a religion in any capacity. None. Zero. Nada. In no capacity was Jesus, in any form, tied into religion. Which is probably why he angered religious people to the point that they wanted to kill him (which they eventually did!).

When Jesus disappeared in Jerusalem at twelve years old, he was in the temple debating the religious leaders. Yes, he was likely teaching them things from the Torah, but not from a religious perspective; instead, kingdom things. The leaders were astonished. Every twelve-year-old Jewish boy had the knowledge of the Torah, but the way Jesus was bringing it to them blew them away.

This is why, later, Jesus taught his disciples:

Pray, then, in this way:
Our Father, who is in heaven,
Hallowed be Your name.
Your kingdom come.
Your will be done,
On earth as it is in heaven.

Matthew 6:9-10

The word *kingdom* is made up of two words: *King* and *Dominion* or *Domain*. That is why, when we talk about Kingdom, we are talking about the King's domain.

THE LAST ADAM

You have to remember; God never lost the earth when Adam fell; he lost the world (*kosmos*). Two different things. The earth is different than the world. When Satan took Jesus up to a high place and showed him all the kingdoms of the world in a moment's time, Satan said: "These things have been handed over to me and I can do with them whatever I will. If you will bow down and worship me, then I will give them to you."

Jesus said: "No deal, Devil. You will only worship the Lord your God and serve him only. Yes, you are right in some sense. I have come after these kingdoms and I am going to get them, but I am going to get them my Father's way."

That's powerful. Satan knew what Jesus was after, so he offered him what he came after, hoping that he would say, "Let's do it this way."

But Jesus was not going to be like the first Adam; Jesus was not even the second Adam. He was the *last* Adam. He was saying to Satan: "I have got this and I am going to take the kingdoms from you."

Jesus knew that he was the Word; it was he who was spoken of by the Father in Genesis 3:15:

> *And I will make enemies*
> *Of you and the woman,*
> *And of your offspring and her Descendant;*
> *He shall bruise you on the head,*
> *And you shall bruise Him on the heel.*

Satan knew that Jesus was the one who was going to crush his head, so he had nothing to lose in trying to tempt Jesus. He was like a condemned prisoner gambling everything he had to avoid his execution.

Hallelujah! Thank God! Jesus prevailed! That is because Jesus is a kingdom man. Amen! And we are kingdom people.

There are two kingdoms on the earth and *only* two kingdoms. There is the Kingdom of Darkness and the Kingdom of Light. The definition of *darkness* in the Greek is simple. It means "ignorance," not to be confused with *stupid*. "Stupid is as stupid does" (Forest Gump).

The word for *light* in the New Testament is the Greek word for knowledge. So the Kingdom of Darkness is the kingdom of ignorance and the Kingdom of Light is the kingdom of knowledge. Ignorance or Knowledge. Which would you choose?

You and I—if we are born again—are the light of the world. See, when we talk about darkness, we are not talking about evil acts of the enemy. That is the picture that religion has painted us. Religion teaches that *darkness* means evil demons lurking everywhere trying to destroy us, give us bad dreams and causing mayhem in the world. But the word *darkness* means "ignorance." Jesus' offer in his Sermon on the Mount went right to the heart of ignorance:

> *Blessed are those who hunger and thirst for righteousness, for they will be satisfied.*

Matthew 5:6

He was saying that those who are hungry for the truth could come to the light, to the knowledge. And as they came into knowledge, all of their deeds would be manifested and dealt with. Those who stay in darkness love darkness because they do not want their deeds to be known.

KOSMOS

Despite the fact that we love having "a personal savior," Jesus also came for the world (*kosmos*), that which was lost by Adam. John 3:16 tells us as much:

> *For God so loved the world, that He gave His only Son, so that everyone who believes in Him will not perish, but have eternal life.*

Again, the word *world* in the Greek is *kosmos* and it means "order, government and structure." So in essence, John wrote: "God so loved order..."

The word *kosmos* has nothing to do with humanity. Instead, it is referring to governmental order and structure. So God loved order so much that he sent his only begotten son into the disorder to restore order. And whosoever believes in him—his purpose, cause and assignment—will live eternally. The belief that we have our salvation (saved from hell) is not the full extent of what Jesus offers us. There is more to believing in Jesus than getting your ticket to heaven. God's promise comes from believing in the man Jesus. Jesus embodies the cause. Hallelujah!

Certainly, the promise of God is sure:

He came to His own, and His own people did not accept Him. But as many as received Him, to them He gave the right to become children of God, to those who believe in His name, who were born, not of blood, nor of the will of the flesh, nor of the will of a man, but of God.

John 1:11-13

Yet it is not fully understood.

THE CAUSE

When John says "those who believe in his name," he is referring to Jesus' cause. It gives us a prophetic picture of Jesus stepping out of the unseen realm and into the seen realm, bringing the light to a darkened world, declaring "Light, BE!" over a formless and desolate emptiness. It is the knowledge of the Father manifesting something in our hearts that is in the Father's heart.

Therefore, when He comes into the world, He says, "You have not desired sacrifice and offering, but you have prepared a body for Me;"

Hebrews 10:5

For You do not delight in sacrifice
Otherwise I would give it;
You do not take pleasure in burnt offering.
The sacrifices of God are a broken spirit;
A broken and a contrite heart, God
You will not despise.

Psalm 51:16-17

In the beginning was the Word, and the Word was with God, and the Word was God.

And the Word became flesh, and dwelt among us.

John 1:1, 14

Jesus stepped out of the unseen realm and into the seen realm to manifest the heart of the Father, and in so doing he redeemed the disorder, placing it back into order. Jesus said,

> And Jesus came up and spoke to them, saying, "All authority in heaven and on earth has been given to Me. Go, therefore, and make disciples of all the nations, baptizing them in the name of the Father and the Son and the Holy Spirit, teaching them to follow all that I commanded you; and behold, I am with you always, to the end of the age."

> Matthew 28:18-20

All authority in heaven and on earth! So go disciple nations! Amazing! None of this has even a hint of religiousness to it. No odor of the flesh or religion. It is all kingdom; it is governmental.

OWNER

Now, when we use the word *kingdom*, there has to be another word after to identify what that kingdom is. For example, we have the Kingdom of Great Britain. Clearly, we know from the title what kingdom we are talking about.

Here is a story to illustrate this point. My wife, Joan, and I had an American missionary couple stay in Hawaii with us for a short time. They were missionaries in Morocco, a country that is a kingdom with a king.

One day, the couple was standing at the train station as they did most every day, getting ready to carry out their daily activities. Except the train did not come. They waited for several hours and the train never arrived. Finally, they asked someone, "Where is the train?"

"Well, the King is using it today," replied the person.

"Does the king know we have things to do?" they said.

(Sounds like a typical American, doesn't it?)

"You do not understand," said the Moroccan. "That is the King's train, and that is the King's track. And we get to use it when he's not using it."

And that is the way it is. In a kingdom, the king owns everything; everything is his. As a matter of fact, the Word says:

For by Him all things were created, both in the heavens and on earth, visible and invisible, whether thrones, or dominions, or rulers, or authorities—all things have been created through Him and for Him.

Colossians 1:16

Regarding His plan of the fullness of the times, to bring all things together in Christ, things in the heavens and things on the earth.

Ephesians 1:10

We are not called to religion. We are called to kingdom—God's kingdom. That's why it's called "the Kingdom of God." It is not about you or me; it is about the King. Everything in this life is about the King. All of it. Let that take a load off of you. We have tried to make life about us and found out the hard way that it's not about us. It is about God. This is why all things are provided to us when we seek...honor...operate in the King's kingdom. This is the heart of Jesus' teaching:

But seek first His kingdom and His righteousness, and all these things will be provided to you.

Matthew 6:33

BAPTISM UNTO REPENTANCE

When John the Baptist was out in the wilderness baptizing, (whoever named him must have been prophetic, right?), he told the Jews to repent. What does *repent* mean? "To change the way you are thinking, change your mind, change the way you relate to God." John the Baptist was telling the Jews: "You have to repent and change the way you relate to God, because what you are doing in the temple no longer applies to you. It is not going to be valid any longer because the Kingdom of God is at hand. Jesus is coming; light is coming; the Kingdom of God is at hand."

That was enough to wreck any religious person's life, especially in a society built on the Jewish religion.

Of course, John was more than a Baptist; he was a rabbi—a master teacher. And every master teacher had a way of identifying his message, his school of thought with his disciples. John's means of identifying his adherents was baptism. Repentant people would walk into the river, go under (one assumes full immersion; he was a Baptist after all, lol) and come up, having just publicly announced their full commitment to John's kingdom message. John would witness that baptism and in essence certify it. John did not baptize as we do it today, by quoting a profession of faith: "My dear brother or sister, I now baptize you by the authority given to me in the name of the Father, the Son, and the Holy Spirit." John's role was not to recite religious words. Rather, John was the witness (ref. Acts 8:26-39.)

When Jesus came walking into the river, however, John had a different witness:

Behold, the Lamb of God who takes away the sin of the world!

John 1:29

Notice John's words. Was *sin* plural or singular? Singular! "Takes away the *sin*..." What sin? The rebellion of the world. What is the world? The *kosmos*, the system, the government structure. Jesus took away the rebellion of the world. He is restoring order. He baptizes with the Holy Spirit and fire. He makes a way open to us so the governor of the earth—the caretaker of the earth—can come back and live in the temple that is each and every one of us. Yes, Jesus is personal, but his work in each of us is to establish the kingdom, and in so doing, building us together as the world-transforming Kingdom of God.

Now He was questioned by the Pharisees as to when the kingdom of God was coming, and He answered them and said, "The kingdom of God is not coming with signs that can be observed; nor will they say, 'Look, here it is!' or, 'There it is!' For behold, the kingdom of God is in your midst."

Luke 17:20-21

John's reaction to seeing the Lamb of God wading toward him was telling: "No, Jesus you need to baptize me."

Jesus understood better, however: "No, you need to baptize me."

And so, John did. Why? So that when John found himself headed elsewhere, the people would know that Jesus adhered to the master rabbi John. People would identify the locust-eating guy's message, which was the Kingdom of God, with this long-haired, sandaled guy who turned water into wine at weddings and spoke of God as his Father.

And we see in Matthew that after John was taken into custody, Jesus continued with John's message, using it for a platform for his own message.

> From that time Jesus began to preach and say, "Repent, for the kingdom of heaven is at hand."

> Matthew 4:17

That is beautiful. Standing in the water, waiting to be baptized, Jesus was not asking John to conform to *his* message. Rather, Jesus bought into John's message and was publicly baptized into the message to start his own ministry. It was a seamless flow of God, one work building upon the other.

John the Baptist did not preach the destruction of the world. He was not a lunatic hippie hoisting a sign "The End Is Near!" John's message paved the way for the savior of the world. He prepared the soil for the master gardener, the restorer, the fulfillment of the great commission in Genesis.

> For God did not send the Son into the world to judge the world, but so that the world might be saved through Him.

> John 3:17

THE MESSAGE

God did not send his Son into the world to condemn the world (*the structure, the order*) but that the *order* might be saved. God wanted his governmental structure restored. He did not want a religion restored; indeed, he never had one. He wanted his governmental structure back.

When Jesus resurrected, as recorded in the book of Acts, he was still about his Father's business:

> *The first account I composed, Theophilus, about all that Jesus began to do and teach, until the day when He was taken up to heaven, after He had given orders by the Holy Spirit to the apostles whom He had chosen. To these He also presented Himself alive after His suffering, by many convincing proofs, appearing to them over a period of forty days and speaking of things regarding the kingdom of God.*

Acts 1:1-3

Jesus talked to people, demonstrating many convincing proofs over a period of 40 days, discussing things concerning the Kingdom of God before he finally ascended. This reflects Paul in his last days on earth:

> *Now Paul stayed two full years in his own rented lodging and welcomed all who came to him, preaching the kingdom of God and teaching things about the Lord Jesus Christ with all openness, unhindered.*

Acts 28:30-31

People came to Paul daily and he taught them about the Kingdom of God, speaking to them of Jesus the Christ...*unhindered!* Isn't that good? If anyone deserved to teach unhindered, it was Paul. We have a great blessing in this country today in that we can preach relatively unhindered. Let us fight to preserve it.

God is changing our theology today. He is bringing us out of religion and into a place of identifying with him as sons and daughters. Although we call ourselves Christians, it was originally a derogatory term. Scripture records its use as a negative term. God never referred to believers as Christians. How did he refer to us? As sons and daughters, royal priests, ambassadors, the ekklesia. Those are labels we need to take up. Why? Because they give us our true identity.

Now, when we talk about being sons, it speaks of humankind. It is not gender-specific; *sons* includes women. So, both male and female are sons because the word *son* means "mature" in the scripture. The word *child* meant "immature" in Galatians 4. And that was no different from a slave.

When Adam fell, he did not lose a religion. He lost rulership. He lost *radah* (Hebrew). Adam lost a kingdom, and the enemy claimed that kingdom.

> *And he led Him up and showed Him all the kingdoms of the world in a moment of time. And the devil said to Him, "I will give You all this domain and its glory, for it has been handed over to me, and I give it to whomever I want.*

Luke 4:5-6

Fortunately, Jesus didn't take the bait. He didn't fall for the devil's tactics of negotiation.

So where are we now? Well...a better question to ask is: Where *should* we be today? Here's what Jesus told us as he was preparing to leave the earth:

> *This gospel of the kingdom will be preached in the whole world as a testimony to all nations, and then the end will come.*

Matthew 24:14

THE END?

Now let's ask a difficult question about today. Has the gospel of the kingdom been preached to all nations? Certainly, we have done a lot of preaching all over the world. But if you had to label it, what would you call that which has been preached to all the nations? The gospel of the kingdom...or religion?

We have been preaching religion, a subset of which is the gospel of salvation. We have tried to get people to repent of their sins so they could go to heaven. We have been selling fire insurance. That's fine as far as it goes, but it doesn't go far. In the denomination I was raised in, they could preach you out of hell, but they couldn't preach you into the Kingdom of God. Still, I am thankful for my raising; they gave us all they had. I learned more scripture there than most people I know who were raised in other denominations.

Clearly, Jesus has assigned us to preach the gospel of the kingdom, the King and his dominion. The royal sovereignty of King Jesus will be preached into the nations of the world as a testimony to all the nations. And then...the end will come.

We have a lot of work to do. I am a missionary at heart. My grandfather was a missionary, my uncle was a missionary, it runs in my blood. I know I have studied a lot of places missionaries have gone, first Hawaii, being one of those places where missionaries went from America and they took the gospel of religion and the gospel of salvation and they turned many people away from God. The missionaries planted thorn-dropping mesquite trees—an invasive species—on the beaches so the native people would not walk barefooted. Why? The missionaries believed it was a sin to walk barefooted.

Now, some would say: "Well, great. What does that have to do with us today?"

The fact is, our Western church has polluted the churches of the world with thorny issues of their own. Prohibitions on women in ministry, divorced people kicked out of churches, bans on musical instruments, and strict dress codes are examples of the religious trappings deposited on the shores of foreign countries in the name of Christianity.

We have much to undo, and we must do it with the wisdom of the Spirit of God. We must address our past and change beliefs and practices that are not scriptural. We have misshaped nations in Jesus name, causing them to see God in ways that distorts who God really is.

Religion has made God this great big old angry guy up in the heavens with a stick and a long beard, and he's waiting to give us lickings when we mess up. That is not our Father. Not at all.

Yet when we read scriptures like Matthew 24, we interpret them as a mandate to go into every nation, preach to the people that they must get born again, and tell them they will go to heaven when they die... and in the meantime, stop walking barefoot, put on some clothing, and for God's sake kill that incessant drumming.

Religion reads Jesus' words as God watching the "soul counter," that when we preach to the right quantity of the world's population, hopefully getting some saved in the process, Jesus will return and sweep us out of here before the big melee called the tribulation.

Folks, that is not scriptural. (There's another word for it, but this book is rated PG, lol).

Matthew 24 is telling us that we must preach the gospel of the kingdom. The kingdom is life itself. And the King is the central component of the kingdom. He embodies the essence of the kingdom. Everything the kingdom has comes from Jesus.

The Kingdom of God is here. The King is here. We are kings under the King. We are anointed to go forth and be who he created us to be. He never gave us a religion. He gave us a government. That is hard to hear if you've never heard it before, but it is truth. Religion has no part in our lives. We are sons and daughter of the King. Amen.

9

Warfare

RELIGION WILL TELL YOU THAT CHRISTIANS ARE THE ARMY OF THE LORD. "Onward Christian soldiers, marching as to war!" is a stirring hymn but poor theology.

Let's be clear. We are not the army of the Lord in any capacity. In scripture, we are never referred to as God's army. Of course, people say: "Didn't Paul call Timothy a 'good soldier?'" Well, not exactly. Here's what Paul said:

You therefore, my son, be strong in the grace that is in Christ Jesus. And the things that you have heard from me among many witnesses, commit these to faithful men who will be able to teach others also. You therefore must endure hardship as a good soldier of Jesus Christ. No one engaged in warfare entangles himself with the affairs of this life, that he may please him who enlisted him as a soldier.

2 Timothy 2:1-4

Paul told Timothy to endure hardship *as* a good soldier, to have the capacity that a soldier would have. Yet nowhere does God refer to believers as his army. God's army is actually the angelic hosts. That word *host* means "army." It is the military piece of the Kingdom of God. When we go out to the battlefield, we go as sons and daughters of the King. We are kings; we are not an army. And when we go forth as kings, we are not going to fight in a traditional sense. Rather, we fight like kings fight.

Our weapons are declarations, decrees and prophetic words that release the army of God. The enemy should see kings on the battlefield, not a sea of foot soldiers, sergeants, lieutenants, and a few generals, but kings united in releasing the decrees of the Lord.

As kings, we do not run to the battlefield without first coming from the throne of heaven with righteous decrees to release. One of the mistakes we make in spiritual warfare is that we run after the devil, binding, casting out, loosening, and doing all of that stuff that we were taught by well-meaning leaders. Unfortunately, these actions are unhealthy and dangerous, as they can incur significant backlash.

Ever wonder why, when people talk about going into spiritual warfare, they say that all hell broke loose? It's because they did not have a legal right to do what they did, and this in turn gave the enemy legal right to counterattack. These people meant well, but they were ill-prepared. You acquire a legal right to spiritual warfare when you come out of the judicial system of heaven with a righteous decree from the Righteous Judge on your behalf. Then when you go to the battlefield, the word of the Lord is stronger than any action of the enemy.

This is what Dutch Sheets refers to when he talks about our appeal to heaven. Some call it the courts of heaven. The teaching varies in some ways, but the essence is that, before we run to the battlefield in spiritual warfare, we have to be before the throne of God. Our part of the Kingdom of God on earth does not come when we release what we want to see happening on earth. Oh, we can get vocal and sound impressive. But the strength for real, positive, productive results comes from releasing what is in Father's heart. And to get that, we have to go to the Father.

Yes, Jesus seemed to offer broad latitude when he said in John 14:13:

If you ask anything in My name, I will do it.

But remember: who was he speaking to? He was speaking to his seasoned disciples who had been with him for three years. They understood (or were beginning to understand) how to exercise that promise. Jesus trusted them. They knew the parameters upon which that promise was based. This was not a promise for fledglings and certainly not a promise for unbelievers.

As kings, when we engage the enemy by decreeing the righteous judgments God has given us, we can see the release of the angelic host—the army of God—to enforce what we have decreed, which are God's strategies.

Recall the difference between the Kingdom of Heaven and the Kingdom of God. The Kingdom of Heaven is the entire sphere, fully under God's authority and conforming to the law and the order of the King of Heaven. The Kingdom of God is the territory presently coming into conformance with the Kingdom of Heaven.

This is why Jesus said of the Father:

Your kingdom come.
Your will be done
On earth as it is in heaven.

Matthew 6:10

Jesus was teaching us that everything in heaven has to be filtered through something on the earth. The Kingdom of Heaven is the home country. The Kingdom of God is the territory; it is owned by the Creator. Yes, the earth is the Lords:

The earth is the Lord's, and all it contains,
The world, and those who live in it.

Psalm 24:1

But it needs to be conformed to the laws, authority and dominion of the Creator. It is a work in progress.

The Kingdom of God is the result of heaven's influence on the earth. This occurs many different ways, but in large part it comes through the Ekklesia. Now, the Ekklesia is not the Kingdom of God. Rather, it is a part of the Kingdom of God.

The greatest obstacle to the Kingdom of God is religion. Misplaced and misguided religious passion has left lasting scars in the history of civilization. Consider the crusades, the inquisitions, the Salem witch trials, the holocaust, to name a few of the religion-driven atrocities inflicted upon the earth.

Why is religion such a powerful controlling force? Why does Islam, Buddhism, Hinduism, Judaism and offshoots of Christianity attract adherents who would die for their religion and kill others for the same? The answer goes beyond a political, cultural or social ideology. Something gets deep into people's soul. It warps their sense of reality and drives aberrant behavior.

Of course, any belief structure will change a person. When we orient our hearts toward a core set of beliefs, a spiritual transaction occurs in that direction. The act of believing is to open ourselves on a deep level, and to receive what is at the core of those beliefs. We open ourselves to the spiritual energy of it and receive it. This begins to change us. This is how religion changes people. Remarkably, it is also how the Kingdom of God changes people. The difference is the Kingdom of God changes people in the direction of loving each other. It makes us Christ-like.

An exchange of spiritual energy changes the soul of a person. Now, some teachers say your soul is bad, your spirit is perfect, and man is inherently evil. I do not agree with such teaching. The evil that manifests in our lives—and we all experience that to some degree—is learned throughout life. Babies are not born scheming evil things, are they? Yes, they cry, fuss, and later throw fits, but that is because they are hungry, confused, frustrated or lonely. Little humans are born pure. They acquire many things as they grow up, good things and bad things. This is one reason we all need Jesus.

Religious practices over thousands of years leave an imprint that is difficult to overcome. There is a comfort to ritual and tradition. Being a Roman Catholic, for example, is easy if your family has been Roman Catholic since Constantine's corruption. It is the same for any established religion, and tradition isn't all negative. It can become so when the spirit of religion, which is active in many religious practices, begins to affect how we view truth. It is difficult for a religious person to read the Bible clearly. Their interpretation will be skewed, shaped by generations of doctrine and practice. Even moral choices become warped with the justification: "Well, God told me this is right."

Their God is operating through the spirit of religion. At that point, the argument is not between right and wrong. It is between who is God and who is not.

There are two major strongmen operating in the world—a political spirit and a religious spirit. The enemy really does not care which one you are serving as long as you are serving one of them. Often, the political spirit functions like the religious spirit. The same passions are aroused; the same "save the world" idealism is enflamed; the same justifications are used for corrupt behavior

Now, does that mean we should not be involved in the things that are going on in our government? Quite the contrary. We should be involved! We must get involved in these things and send kingdom people into these areas of influence. My point is to identify how a religious spirit and a political spirit controls our society.

A good example is the democrat party today in the US. I realize people have differing viewpoints on political and social issues, and that is healthy. Nobody sees things the same. Nobody is completely right. But when I was young, the democrats were the ones preaching peace, love, tolerance and freedom of expression. Today...not so much. It is actually a religion now. It is a form of demonic worship, and socialism, humanism and Marxism are at the core of it. Satanic practices have replaced the once wholesome values of the party.

Whatever door we leave open for the enemy will soon be filled with the enemy. This is why Jesus does not want to be a part of your life. He wants to be the entirety of your life. Everything in your life should flow through him: your ideology, philosophy and theology, and this should flow from his kingship. When we flow with Jesus, there is no room for a political spirit or a religious spirit. Deception cannot stand when confronted with the authentic truth that is Jesus Christ.

God is confronting us. He is challenging us. Whenever we become swayed by things not of him, he checks us by the Holy Spirit. We are living in the day when we have to stand up and be the voice of the kingdom. We cannot bend to what others want us to do.

The Kingdom of God is not a theory; it is a lifestyle. It requires bold people in our country, all the way down to the local level, to stand for righteousness. Why would God call us to such dedication? Doesn't he just want us to get people saved and going to heaven? Well...that's important, but that's not the kingdom message. The goal is not to get people into heaven. Why does heaven need more people? The goal is getting heaven to the earth where it's needed.

God loves nations. In Matthew 28, Jesus tells us to disciple nations. God has a plan for all nations. Yet when you and I, kingdom people, sons and daughters of God, pull back and say we should not be involved in government or social things, we are refusing to play a part in God's purposes in redeeming this nation.

We have a heavenly responsibility to be engaged in the country we live in. Our vote is our voice; it is heard when we hold accountable those who are in office. We do so through our vote and other's votes. Remember the prophetic word from Robert Hunt at Cape Henry in 1607, when he planted the cross:

> The gospel of the kingdom will go into this new land and from
> its shores, the gospel of the kingdom will go to the nations of
> the world.

That is part of our prophetic destiny as a country, and there are things that are being put in place right now that are contrary to that plan—the equality act, for one. If we are not making noise about that, we need to start now. We cannot surrender by saying "Well, they are going to pass it anyway because people are silent." We have to pray. Yes. But there is also a time to put feet to our prayers. Amen!

It is time to make phone calls. It is time to get people active. God has called you and me to steward this earth. We do so by stewarding our nations, states, communities, cities, neighborhoods and families. As we steward the places God has given us, the change we desire will become a God-given reality. But it requires kingdom people doing their part.

I believe abortion could be overturned very easily in this nation if kingdom people would rise up. It breaks God's heart. It is an abomination. It is the shedding of innocent blood. I don't know how somebody who says they believe in Jesus can support such a horrible practice. I don't know how they can support a political party that has abortion as part of their platform. The rationale that says: "Well, I vote the person, not the party" is bull dung. Elected officials always conform to the platform of their party. When you give people your vote, you are attaching yourself to that platform.

Throughout scripture, we have responsibilities. Nations are judged not because of what the wicked are doing but because of what the righteous are doing...or not doing. God is not going to judge America because of the ungodly. The ungodly are merely doing a better job being wicked than the church is doing being kingdom people. Our job is not to defeat them, but to win them for the kingdom. We have a responsibility to step up to action and engage our culture.

I know...it is inconvenient. You put yourself out there. You get exposed to a lot of stuff. People attack you any way they can. My wife, Joan, ran for the statehouse in Hawaii twice. Now, I understand that she might not appeal to every voter; no one does. But folks, we received death threats. We had people vandalize our property. People got up in our face. That is stuff a redneck should not have to deal with because you respond differently when you're from Mississippi. I had to put a good bit of my redneckian tendencies under my feet when I really wanted to put some people under my feet. But I did good, praise God. I didn't hit anybody...except in my mind, and I repented of that later.

But let me tell you, people are willing to die for their social views and political views just as they are for their religious beliefs, and they are happy to take you with them. Why? Because most of these things are controlled by spiritual entities.

We were living in Hawaii at the time, and the thing that caused Joan to run for office was a prophetic word. We found ourselves involved in the same-sex marriage fight. We went to our legislators, our representatives and senators, and we reminded them that the people of Hawaii had voted to define marriage as between one man and one woman. The people did not want elected leaders making these decisions outside of the voting booth, and they brought it up again. This was during Obama's tenure, and we wound up having 20,000 people come to the state capital and demand their voices be heard on the issue.

That is a lot of folks, and it made the politicians nervous. Out of this, Joan decided to run for office. It was about the voice of the people that was being silenced. It was about the established politicians taking the vote away, taking the right away, just as it is today. If you let the American people do what is right and live within their rights, we would have far fewer problems.

In spite of the will of the people, the politicians went ahead and voted for same-sex marriage to be legal in the state of Hawaii. That's when the Lord said, "I want you now to put your money where your mouth is."

We were shocked. "Oh my God! What does that mean?"

God answered this way: "I want Joan to run for office."

And she did. She ran twice. And we believe she won twice. We have proof of cheating, but the system prevailed...this time. In the aftermath, however, 13 pastors stepped up and ran for office, all because a little brown woman who was not even born in America—Joan is a naturalized citizen from the Philippines—stepped up and ran for the statehouse. Many awakened believers came to us later and said they were embarrassed that it took somebody that was not even Hawaiian or born in our nation to take action before they did it.

I thought: *Yes Lord, this is awesome. You are shaking the state and the church.* Joan's race will set the tone of the political climate of Hawaii for decades to come. The church is now more involved in government and politics than any other time in history. From that first year, from the lieutenant governor all the way down to neighborhood boards, people were stepping out and saying that Joan inspired them to run.

Let that be said about you! Run! Put your name out there. Let people see what you believe in and what you stand for. You may say: "Well, that is not my calling. I am a preacher. I am a pastor. I am a this or that."

Do you realize that many of the founding fathers were ministers? Some had led churches during the revolutionary war. They would come to church, pull their pistols from their holsters and lay them on the pulpits, preach the gospel of the kingdom, take off their black robes, take back their pistols, and lead the men of their congregation to fight for freedom.

They were called the Black-Robed regiment. Men like John Muhlenberg, James Cadwell and Jonas Clark understood that:

"There's a time of war, and a time of peace. There is a time for all things: a time to preach and a time to pray. But there is also a time to fight, and that time has now come!"

John Muhlenberg

Those guys had grit. Today we have girly men in skinny jeans running churches with sound systems, strobe lights and smoke machines.

Some might say: "Why do we have to get involved? Won't God just show up and change everything?"

Hell, no! God will only change things *through* us, because anytime God wants to do anything on the earth, he needs a person to do it. That's why Jesus came in the flesh. God could have just changed things sovereignly. But that's not the system he established. Incidentally, this system works both ways. Anytime the devil wants to do something on the earth, he also needs a person to do it. And he's got a bunch of them right now.

God is looking for a company of men and women who will rise up and say: "I will lead the charge in my city, my state, my nation! And I will be a part of what God uses to take my government back! In Jesus' name!"

Now, please don't disqualify yourself before you even start. Do not say: "I am not qualified to do that."

It doesn't matter if you have a third-grade education. You will be taught how to govern. There are classes and training for you to go through after you get elected. You don't have to be the smartest person in the room; you just have to know smart people. And that starts with Jesus Christ!

My brother Andy was elected judge in the state of Mississippi, and they put him through class despite having no law degree, just a passion for justice. He was the youngest judge ever elected in the State of Mississippi, being elected at age 29. He served two terms as judge, then he ran, and won his race for sheriff in Monroe County, Mississippi.

Let yourselves be challenged! Allow your social views to be shaped by kingdom values, and do not be afraid to promote them in society. Religious beliefs, political beliefs and social views have moved people to give their lives for their positions. Can we do the same for the kingdom? The Book of Revelation tells us:

Then I heard a loud voice in heaven, saying,

"Now the salvation, and the power, and the kingdom of our God and the authority of His Christ have come, for the accuser of our brothers and sisters has been thrown down, the one who accuses them before our God day and night. And they overcame him because of the blood of the Lamb and because of the word of their testimony, and they did not love their life even when faced with death."

Revelation 12:10-11

"They did not love their life even when faced with death." That is important for us. See, unless we engage and get involved, we are not going to see our nations changed. Prayer alone is not enough. Now, a religious mindset says: "Oh yes, it is. God is just going to do it if we pray enough."

Let me tell you, God is sovereignly moving in our nation through you and me and everyone who responds to the kingdom message. But he's doing it with us, not in spite of us. Folks, if you haven't figured out by now, the goal is not the earth. Not really. God has lots of planets. The goal is the maturation of the sons and daughters of God. That is the kingdom. That is why God is not going to do it for us. Our job is our maturation. Jesus is returning for a mature bride.

It is a universal hunger that we face. Every culture, no matter how old or how far removed from God, has developed some form of religious practice that attempts to satisfy the vacuum in the pit of the human soul. You can look in any of the remote parts of the earth and find religious practices there. Why? Because religion is a spirit, and much of it requires human life sacrifice. In the Philippines, headhunters and cannibals operated through a pagan religious worship. I met one or two of them.

This is what we are up against. But if we come in with the gospel of the kingdom, we can shift every culture, every ethnos, every nation, every people group. If we think our message will not work in the jungles of South America and Africa and the South Pacific—if we think it only works in America—then it is a Western theology and it should not be taught. Our message must work in every corner of the earth. We are not called to change Western civilization. We are called to change the world.

The world is in a vacuum, crying out for reason, purpose, eternal significance. The Kingdom of God gives us all of those things, and sacrifice has already been made.

10

Who Are You?

WE WERE CREATED BY GOD FOR MORE THAN MERE EXISTENCE. Each and every one of us was created to live a fulfilled and significant life. That's kingdom. Religion would have us put on hairshirts and suffer our way into heaven. That's not why God put us on earth. We are called to full and productive lives, bearing witness to the King of kings and establishing his kingdom. The goal is not to die old but to die empty, having given all we could give. Life is life, and it is in God's hands.

> *Your eyes have seen my formless substance;*
> *And in Your book were written*
> *All the days that were ordained for me,*
> *When as yet there was not one of them.*

Psalm 139:16

God has our days written in a book. Personally, I'm praying for 120 years, if God wants to give it to me. I'd love to have it. I'm not looking to leave today because I know our assignment's here. But when we leave the earth, we are to leave empty. Give all you have. Leave it all on the field.

Jesus lived 33 years; he was not that old. He died at 33 but he did not die unfulfilled. He did not die out of his purpose. He died emptied. He left everything on the cross. When we can live life to empty instead of old, we'll start living out of our purpose. Let this challenge you. Live to empty. This strikes at the heart of all human pursuit.

Just as mankind was not created to suffer death, we were also not created for worship. Sure, we have hymn books, songs and worship leaders that broadcast far and wide the doctrine that our exclusive purpose is to worship God. But the truth is, we were not created for worship. We were created for rulership. And out of our purposeful kingdom living comes worship, longevity, fulfillment and significance. It's a matter of priorities.

Many folks like to quote the verse saying God inhabits the praises of his people (ref. Psalm 22:3 KJV). That's certainly one of our assignments. Yet that does not mean that God likes it when we get the band together and sing worship songs. The Hebrew translation of Psalm 22:3 is revealing. That verse is really saying: "God inhabits the life of a man who produces praise." It's not using the word *worship*, it's *praise*. And what does God inhabit? "The life of a man." So the real meaning of this is that as you walk through life, you are producing worship and praise to the Lord out of your life, doing and being who God created you to be. Even if you can't carry a tune.

God inhabits the praises of his people through their kingdom lives. As you go through life, whether you're in government, business, ministry, arts and entertainment, driving a garbage truck or teaching kids, your life of kingdom purpose releases worship and praise to God.

Man is the crowning act of an intentional Creator. We are his magnum opus. Hebrews tells us we were made just lower than God.

> *What is man, that You think of him?*
> *Or a son of man, that You are concerned about him?*
> *You have made him for a little while lower than angels;*
> *You have crowned him with glory and honor;*
> *You have put everything in subjection under his feet.*

Hebrews 2:6-8

Now, many people have been taught this passage out of the King Jimmy version, which says "a little lower than the angels." That's incorrect, however. The word used here is *Elohim*, not *angels*. We are not made lower than angels. We're a little lower than Elohim—God himself.

Let that liberate you. We are not the crumbs from the master's table. We are in the chain of command: the Father, the Son, the Holy Spirit, then us! It has been taught that angels are just below the

Godhead, but that's not true. It's us. Amazing! Yet we live so far beneath our God-given positioning. We're letting demons have authority on the earth. The fact is, they have no authority unless man gives it to him.

What would the earth look like if we stepped up into the kingly and priestly anointing that God has given us—his sons and daughters—and began to govern where God has placed us? It would look like the Kingdom of God! So, how do we do that? How do we govern like that? How do we kingdom?

Let's examine what it is like when God ushers you into a sphere of influence. The first thing you need to do is say, "Father, what is your heart for this place?"

Most people, when they go into a job, are thinking: *Okay I'm going here to make a living.* That's not kingdom thinking. From the perspective of the Kingdom of God, you are working to bring life. All your education, all of your training and experience, everything you've ever done, has brought you into a sphere of influence to bring the Kingdom of God.

Now, when you get there, don't say, "Well, how am I going to change this situation?" Don't grab that 14-pound family Bible off your coffee table and walk in to work the first day like the new sheriff here to clean up Dodge City. No, please don't do that. What do you do? First thing you do is pray. Ask the Father:

- Why am I here?
- Why am I in this business?
- Why am I in this branch of this business?
- Why am I in this city with this business?
- Why have I birthed a business in this city?
- What is God's heart for this place in which he has placed me?

Then take time to hear from the Father. He will download your purpose and you will begin to understand your purpose for being there. As you pursue your purpose, however, you need to do so diplomatically. And diplomatically doesn't mean *soft*; it means carefully. Don't fear making mistakes; you've got diplomatic immunity.

> *What then shall we say to these things? If God is for us, who is against us?*
>
> Romans 8:31

If you wreck a few things, if you make some mistakes, you've still got diplomatic immunity. Praise God.

Then, after: "Father, what do you want to do?" now you ask: "Father, how do we implement this?"

Notice the operative word *we*. See, embedded in the asking is a prophetic spirit at work. Our questions stir God's heart to release his Spirit. Grace comes from the cry of our hearts. Our questions qualify us to receive the Father's response. This is important for many reasons. Sometimes we just need to get the full picture before setting forth on a course of action.

For example, when I'm prophesying to someone, I'm always listening to the Father. I'm not just asking what God wants to say to the person, but I'm also asking: "Father, how do I articulate what I'm hearing?"

See, in prophecy, you don't always say everything you hear. Some of what you hear is to help you articulate what this person needs. So, the question becomes: "Father, how do I say this so that it hits this person's spirit and it makes them come alive?"

The person receiving the word will hear the Lord in my words even though it might sound crazy to anyone else. But the words, the phrases, even the emphasis on the syllables will impact the person right where God wants to reach them. That's the way you do it.

As you impact the region God has you in, remember that the language you use should not be Christianese. Why? Because people don't understand that dialect. We are God's crowning act. Now we must learn to act like it.

How did Jesus act? Did he spend all of his time in the temple discussing the Old Testament with a bunch of gray beards? No. He was a friend of sinners. He spent his ministry life among the people who needed him and would respond to him. That tells us something. We need to be hanging out with sinners more than each other. We need to go to where the harvest is.

When we come to Christ, religion says: "Come out of the world; you're to be among them but not of them; come out of the world. Come gather in your little buildings and worship God, and pray and intercede. Believe God to move."

Sounds holy, doesn't it? Unfortunately, if the enemy can get you to believe that lie, you'll never see your city change, because you'll be under a church roof praying and believing God for people you will never know or understand. Prayer is important; so is human contact.

Jesus knew where the harvest was, and it wasn't in religion. When he got around temple folks, he either got in trouble or he caused trouble. Still, it doesn't help that he turned over tables, drove merchants from the temple with a whip, called religious people names (scribes, pharisees, hypocrites!), insulted their religious views with "blasphemy," and made fools of them in the eyes of the common people. This is not how to win friends and influence people. Instead of the denizens of the temple, Jesus got along best with prostitutes, drunkards, tax collectors (notorious for their greed and corruption), rough-hewn fishermen and lunatics—people for whom the religious world was a foreign environment.

That is our example. If you are a believer in Christ, you are made for the same environment, not to conform to it, but to transform it. Notice I said "transform it," and not "correct it." What good does it do to correct people every time they drop the F-bomb? Oh, it offends you? Tough. Put on your big-boy britches and get in the thick of it. If they use the name of the Lord in vain, roll with it. They're heathens. That's their dialect. It's nothing personal to God. If God can take it and still love them, so can you.

Of course, if a believer continually talks like that, you might want to have a one-on-one conversation with them. But don't bring them before the church. Pull them aside. "Hey, Brother Smith / Sister Jane, can I help you with some better vocabulary here?" But if you hear heathens doing it, don't let it rub you the wrong way. Why? Because they're being good heathens. And they need you in their lives, not to condemn them or to show them that they're sinners. They already know they're sinners. They're good at it, and some are even proud of it. Yet deep down inside they know they need help. Some of the best sinners I know were once really good sinners. Apostle Paul, anyone? He was out killing believers when God smacked him upside the head and knocked him off his ass. And he thought he was serving God.

In Hawaii, I had my Friend of Sinners Club. It was a coffee shop in our town where a bunch of retired military biker guys and a few old coaches hung out. When I first started going there, I'd think: *Oh, I better be careful. Oh, my Lord. These guys aren't Christians in the slightest!* I had to watch my language. I was a good representative of Jesus, but sitting around in the company of guys for whom every other word was an artful cuss, it was easy to slip into that vernacular. Funny thing was, they knew I led a church, so every time they'd rip off a particularly colorful string of toxic invective, it'd go like this:

"Oh preacher. I'm sorry."

"Men, it don't bother me a bit."

"You don't care if we curse?"

"Nah, men. Do your thing."

And you know what? As time went on and they came to accept me, when they got in trouble, they'd call me for advice. I'd help them and they'd want to repay me somehow. Most of them were religious in some sense. A few were practicing Roman Catholics and others really great heathens. I'd say: "Man, I don't need your money. I need your friendship." And then they would find out we were doing something at the church and they would send money there, or they would buy out our kids when they were fundraising. Why? Because they were in my Friend of Sinners Club. They didn't know that's what I called it. Incredibly, several of those guys got born again. One of them moved onto our church campus. We gave him a place to live, helped him get a job, taught him to live responsibly, got him on his feet. That's Kingdom.

Here's another piece of kingdom. A friend of mine in Texas was a pastor there for a while. He's a rancher, too. Well, a Baptist pastor moved to the region after the sponsor church offered him a position with a salary. When he arrived there, however, the church said they couldn't pay him. (God knows that *never* happens.) So, my friend, who was kingdom minded, leading a kingdom-minded church, reached out to the new pastor and said:

"Hey Pastor, what were they going to pay you?"

"Oh man, I dunno." The pastor thought he was being nosey.

"No, no really. What were they going to pay you?"

The Baptist pastor told him, and my friend said, "I'm going to pay your salary and double it."

And so, my friend's church paid that Baptist preacher's salary— paid him *twice* what the sponsor church promised to pay him. And my friend wound up winning him over as a friend. Later, this Baptist preacher was filled with the Holy Spirit and moved on to his next assignment.

Now, when you read that we are the crowning act of God, let these examples inform you what it really means. If God, as a man, could walk among sinners and be comfortable, even productive, so can you. As a repentant prostitute poured sweet perfume over Jesus' feet and the religious people screamed, he said to leave her alone. Her worship was pure.

Can you see the corrosive effects religion has on us? As we walk away from religion and into the Kingdom of God, we are going to see people who want the love of the King, the love expressed through you as a believer. In time, my sinner's club began to ask me questions: "What kind of church are you a member of?" And I would stimulate their interest with answers like: "I'm not a member of a church because you can't have membership in a country. You can only have *citizenship* in a country."

"Well, aren't you a pastor?"

"No." (In truth, I'm not a pastor.)

"What are you?"

"I'm the leader of that group of people down there."

Sure, I could have browbeat them with information, but instead, I let them ask. Some of them called me an apostle, but I'd correct them: "I'm a son of God." And that blew their minds because they thought there was only one son of God.

The effect my engagement had on those guys was life-changing... for them and for me. Every one of us need one of those clubs. But there are some rules to follow. First, don't go in thinking you are their savior or that you're there to change them. You're only there to love them. And if they want the opportunity to change, they can be introduced to the Son of God who can change them.

Second, if you find yourself being pulled under by the sinful environment, that's an indication that you have no business there. You're simply not equipped. For example, if you find yourself buying shots for the bar and staggering home every night "in Jesus mighty name," there might be some adjustments you need to make. Not every person can function in every sinful environment. You need to know where God is leading you.

The point is, don't expect ministry to be all white steeples and organ music. The harvest is out there beyond the altars and pews. The ripe fields are the hearts of the lost—good people oppressed by the devil through their ignorance. And a light is best seen in darkness.

When Jesus cleansed 10 lepers, he commanded them: "Go and show yourselves to the priests" (ref. Luke 17). As they went, however, one turned back, fell at Jesus' feet and thanked him. The others didn't. And that's okay. Why? Because Jesus is showing us it's not all about us. Some of those we influence will respond by thanking us; others won't.

Don't worry about it. We live our lives unto God. It is to him that they should bring their thanks.

It is essential to understand that before anything was, God is. This is what Jesus meant when he spoke words that enraged the religious establishment.

> *So the Jews said to Him, "You are not yet fifty years old, and You have seen Abraham?"*
>
> *Jesus said to them, "Truly, truly I say to you, before Abraham was born, I am."*
>
> John 8:57-58

SOURCE

What do we mean by *God*? It describes a self-existing one, a self-sufficient one. God had no creator. He is his own creator. When you call God *Father*, do you really know what you're calling him? The Hebrew word for *father* (or *daddy*) is *abba*. The word actually means "source." So when we say *God* or *Father,* we are saying, "Source, I love you. Source, I adore you. Source, I'm thankful for you."

He is the source of everything in life. Father is that to the family. In roles of the family, the father's role is to be the provider for the family. He's the source of everything that your family needs. Everything we have comes through Jesus. The Bible says in John 16 that these things are delivered (or exposed) to us through Holy Spirit:

> *"I have many more things to say to you, but you cannot bear them at the present time. But when He, the Spirit of truth, comes, He will guide you into all the truth; for He will not speak on His own, but whatever He hears, He will speak; and He will disclose to you what is to come.*
>
> John 16:12-13

Notice the word *truth*. It is closely tied to the word *light*. Light is knowledge. This is how Jesus used the term in John 3:

The one who believes in Him is not judged; the one who does not believe has been judged already, because he has not believed in the name of the only Son of God. And this is the judgment, that the Light has come into the world, and people loved the darkness rather than the Light; for their deeds were evil. For everyone who does evil hates the Light, and does not come to the Light, so that his deeds will not be exposed. But the one who practices the truth comes to the Light, so that his deeds will be revealed as having been performed in God."

John 3:18-21

Those who are seekers of truth are people drawn to the light. So, when Jesus talks about knowing truth, he's talking about coming to light, coming into knowledge of Holy Spirit:

He [Holy Spirit] will glorify Me, for He will take from Mine and will disclose it to you.

All things that the Father has are Mine; this is why I said that He takes from Mine and will disclose it to you.

John 16:14-15

"All things that the Father has are mine." How much does the Father have?

Everything.

How much of it belongs to Jesus?

All of it.

How much is Holy Spirit going to show to you?

All of it.

"He takes from Mine and will disclose it to you." Holy Spirit takes it, presents it and gives it to us. This is really mind-boggling. God has everything and he gives us everything for the facilitating of the Kingdom of God. Everything we need for life is already in us because Holy Spirit is in us.

Of course, it doesn't always look that way, does it? We are not living in the fullness of all God gives us. That is what this book (and others like it) are for—to get us to that place of receiving everything the Father has for us, which is... everything... as we align with him.

To receive all that the Father has for us, we must come into alignment with the Father just as Jesus was aligned. We have to get to the place where we are walking like Jesus walked. How did Jesus walk? I'm glad you asked:

> *Therefore Jesus answered and was saying to them, "Truly, truly, I say to you, the Son can do nothing of Himself, unless it is something He sees the Father doing; for whatever the Father does, these things the Son also does in the same way.*

> John 5:19

> *"I have revealed Your name to the men whom You gave Me out of the world; they were Yours and You gave them to Me, and they have followed Your word. Now they have come to know that everything which You have given Me is from You; for the words which You gave Me I have given to them; and they received them and truly understood that I came forth from You, and they believed that You sent Me.*

> John 17:6-8

Jesus did what he saw the Father do. Jesus revealed the Father's name—a name conveys power, authority and honor—and the words Jesus gave his disciples were the Father's words. That's alignment.

Now, that sounds simple, but it's difficult for you and me. Part of our difficulties are the religious excuses we throw up in defense of our spiritual impotency. "We live in the flesh, not the spirit. They war against one another. We struggle as we wait for God to change us." Well... yeah they do, at times. But we get to determine who wins the war. It's not like we're in the stands watching it. We are the battlefield and we determine the outcome.

It is a difficult thing at times to transition out of this religious mindset promising that God is going to transform us in the blink of an eye. *Poof, it's done.* Unfortunately, religion can't be cast out of us. It's there for a reason—it satisfies a need—and it has to be displaced with something better. How do we displace religion? We displace darkness and ignorance with light and knowledge. We learn, we grow, and we surrender. But knowledge itself is not enough. We can fill our heads with knowledge and still make no difference in the world. To be effective for the kingdom, knowledge has to be activated by purpose and passion for our assignment.

Holy Spirit has to be given permission to come into our hearts and possess the throne of our lives. He will be the one who leads us. We don't lead ourselves. We're not our own. Hallelujah! We are his; we are his workmanship; we are on his assignment, and we continually yield to him just as Jesus did.

"Father, what do you want me to do? What do you want me to say? Where do you want me to go?"

Now, some people's approach to this relationship is to become a spaced-out weirdo who can't (or won't) do anything for themselves. "God, when you want me to eat, the plate will just appear." Yeah, these guys are pretty skinny these days. The truth is that we are attached to the Father by way of the Spirit. And we are attached to each other as a body. So we are accountable to God and to one another. Alignment with the Father, then, is alignment with each other.

If you isolate yourself and go do your own thing, you're going to wind up in a religious mold. Jesus showed us how to be connected correctly and how to connect through the scriptures. He gave us apostles, prophets, evangelists, pastors and teachers to equip us to do the work of the ministry. The operative phrase being "to do." These gifts are given for something beyond ourselves. They are for building the body, the church and the Kingdom of God. Still, some folks like titles. They sound impressive. "I'm an apostle. I'm a prophet. I do my own thing. I'm at the top of the food chain."

ACCOUNTABILITY

If you are an apostle, you're not at the top. You're at the bottom, because you're the foundation. Does the foundation go on top? Not unless the purpose is to crush whoever is beneath it. When we approach ministry as Jesus did—as a servant with a washbowl and towel—we get to do what he did.

Apostles in scripture were not isolated mavericks hearing only from God. Consider the Council of Jerusalem when the apostles were gathered from around the known world. We have record that they debated circumcision, among other things. Peter promoted it and Paul opposed it, saying: "Peter, you've missed God." This was how accountability worked in the early church. They were able to debate and confer among themselves and reach consensus when James, the brother of Jesus, said: "Folks, thank you for your input. Here's my decision." See, there was a chief apostle among the apostles, someone that the rest yielded to for the decision. (ref. Acts 15) This was order; this was alignment; this was kingdom.

So, even though there are levels we achieve and ministry we perform on our own, we're never alone nor beyond accountability. The fact is, we'll never be productive if we're not attached to other apostolic people.

Kingdom ministry is all about connection. It's about who we're connected to as an individual in God's army of kings. In God's kingdom, it's about who are we walking with, who are we running with, who we are connected to, who has a voice in our lives.

In the Kingdom of God, we allow people to give us voice as we give them voice into our lives. We do so not out of hierarchy or governmental structure of religion but out of relationship. It's a matter of saying: "You have the right to speak into my life. I want it. And I will speak into yours." This is the synergy of all of the apostolic and prophetic gifts. One can put a thousand of flight, but two can put 10,000 to flight. What we do as an Ekklesia flows from the Source, into our lives and through our lives, and the Kingdom of God expands.

11

The Two Realms

THROUGHOUT OUR STUDY, WE'VE BEEN TALKING ABOUT GOD: the Kingdom of God, hearing from God, aligning with God. Strange as this may seem, however, God is not even his name. It's his description. Because of who he is, he alone qualifies for the title God. He is the source and the creator, and creation bears the mark of the creator. So, when we delve into God's creative process, we must understand not only what he created but who this creator is.

> *For since the creation of the world His invisible attributes, that is, His eternal power and divine nature, have been clearly perceived, being understood by what has been made, so that they are without excuse.*
>
> Romans 1:20

Genesis tells us that God first created the invisible world and then the visible world.

> *In the beginning God created the heavens and the earth. And the earth was a formless and desolate emptiness, and darkness was over the surface of the deep, and the Spirit of God was hovering over the surface of the waters.*
>
> Genesis 1:1-2

Now, remember our questions of inquiry:

- Who is talking?
- Who are they talking to?
- What does it mean in their culture?
- How do we apply this?

We are told that God created the natural universe—all things seen—and that he also created another realm called the supra—the unseen or the supernatural realm. It is vital that we understand the relationship between the two.

In the Hebrew culture, the supernatural realm was not referred to as the spiritual realm. The Hebrews referred to the supernatural realm as the unseen realm and the natural realm as the seen realm.

The natural realm was understood to be integrated with the supernatural realm. Yes, there was a distinction between the two, but the realms where thought to operate together. According to Hebrew thought, if the natural was not integrated with the supernatural, it would be lifeless. Think of a live person compared to a dead body. The live person exists in the natural only as long as they contain spiritual energy. When that energy departs, we have a corpse. Same physical body that we knew before, but lifeless.

Consider what scripture tells us of Jesus' death:

Therefore when Jesus had received this sour wine, he said, "It is finished!" And he bowed his head and gave up his spirit.

John 19:30

Notice that when Jesus gave up his spirit, he died.

Consider also Job 34:14:

If he [God] were to gather his spirit and his breath to himself, humanity would perish together and mankind would return to dust.

The Hebrews knew that no one could fully separate from God's spirit and live; therefore, there is no distinct natural realm apart from the supernatural realm.

God's realm is the supernatural realm, although he operates in both the natural realm (the seen) and the supernatural realm (the unseen), but his place of dwelling is the supernatural realm. Humans exist in the natural realm but we can (and should) operate in the supernatural realm as well as the natural realm. Anyone who has entered the supernatural realm—through worship, praise or prayer—has experienced being in both realms.

Of course, more than God dwells in the supernatural realm. There is evil in the unseen realm, also confusion and conflict and beings that, frankly, couldn't care less. Revelation speaks of a war in heaven (ref. Revelation 12.7). Paul says that our warfare is not in the flesh (the body of the natural realm), but divinely powerful (supernatural) (ref. 2 Corinthians 10:3-4). We can see that just as God comes from the supernatural to the natural, mankind can go from the natural to the supernatural.

For too long, we have thought of the two realms – seen and unseen—as wholly apart from one another. The idea of a separation between a natural realm and a supernatural realm came from ancient Greek thought.

Ancient Greek philosophers taught that the natural realm is below and the supernatural is above. They believed that the supernatural realm was pure and so could not mingle with the impure natural realm. They further posited that God dwells in the supernatural. Since God is perfect, he could not dwell with men, who were imperfect, so a separation must exist. God and man lived apart, and never the twain shall meet.

The Greeks were wrong. Still, like much of Greek culture, the idea of a separation of natural and supernatural is embedded in our western thinking today. The fact is, we think like ancient Greeks. Now, you may say: "I don't think like a Greek. I have never even been to Greece."

It doesn't matter. Greece has been to you. It came through the Roman Catholic Church, among other avenues. Now, you may say: "But I am not Roman Catholic."

It doesn't matter. Roman Catholicism has come to you. The Protestant movement came from the Roman Catholic church. Martin Luther was a Catholic monk before he challenged certain points of Catholicism and eventually separated from the mother church. However, he took a lot of Catholic thinking with him. Because of this, all major protestant denominations have been influenced by the Catholic Church, which took ideas from Greek philosophy.

Hebrew thought is different than Greek thought. They see the natural realm and the supernatural realm superimposed upon one another. They do not see two separate realms. Rather, the two realms are intertwined, dependent on one another, relational.

Recall Jesus' words when he gave Peter the keys to the kingdom:

I will give you the keys of the kingdom of heaven; and whatever you bind on earth shall have been bound in heaven, and whatever you loose on earth shall have been loosed in heaven.

Matthew 16:19

Notice the interaction between earth and heaven. Earth is part of the natural realm. Heaven is a part of the supernatural realm. Nothing is bound or loose in heaven unless it is first done on earth. They work together.

In Exodus 33, as Moses was getting acquainted with the God of the burning bush, he was bold enough to ask this God to show himself more fully. God responded by hiding Moses in the cleft of a rock as he passed by, thereby revealing only his back side because "You cannot see My face, for mankind shall not see Me and live!" (Exodus 33 :17-23).

The significance of this encounter is that God, whom we are told is spirit—actually of spiritual substance (ref. John 4:24)—exists in both realms: natural and spiritual. That is how Moses was able to see the presence of God with his physical eyes.

On the Mount of Transfiguration, where Jesus met with Moses and Elijah, Jesus stepped into another realm. His face shone like the sun and his garments became as white as light. His disciples, Peter and John, who had not transfigured, could see him conversing with Elijah and Moses. This meeting was not in two separate realms. Jesus still had physical substance, yet he interacted within the supernatural realm (ref. Matthew 17:1-3).

The Hebrews, who considered mankind as walking in both realms simultaneously, had no trouble understanding how Moses could see God and how Jesus could hang out with people who had long ago departed the earth. The Hebrews were correct in their view of the integration of the natural and supernatural realms.

Western thinking says that if we are to interact with the supernatural realm, we must do a lot of work to reach it. We need to become ultra-spiritual to enter that realm. It says God must do a spiritual act for us to step into that supernatural realm so we can operate there. That is Greek philosophy and it is wrong.

Hebrew thinking is that the supernatural and the natural are intertwined. This is why Jesus could talk with Moses and Elijah—two deceased guys—and not be judged as Saul was when he reached out to the recently departed Samuel through the Witch of Endor (ref. 1 Samuel 28). Jesus stepped into the unseen realm as the Son of God and caused it to be seen as he talked to the people representing the law and the prophets. This is where we need to walk. More importantly, this is where we have permission to walk—not for the sake of seeing Moses and Elijah, but for the sake of walking as Jesus walked.

Jesus said he did not come to do away with the law and the prophets. He came to fulfill them. On the Mount of Transfiguration, things were transfigured. (They named it well.) The atmosphere was changed, and Jesus conferred with Moses and Elijah representing the law and the prophets. We do not have a record of what they said. Jesus might have said, "Thank you, guys. Give me a high five. I will take it from here. I've fulfilled the law and the prophets." Or maybe it was something else. (Personally, I think he said "Man, wait until Greg Hood writes about this!")

Jesus' disciples who were with him had a different take on what they were seeing. Peter, "Mr. Shoe -leather taster," came up with a great plan: "Lord, it is good that we are here. If you want, I will make three tabernacles here: one for you, one for Moses, and one for Elijah" (Matthew 17:4).

That's when Father God showed up, just as he did at Jesus' baptism. "This is My beloved Son, with whom I am well pleased; listen to Him!"

The Father pretty much set the record straight with that broadcast. The confused disciples would have misused the supernatural experience that Jesus gave them the privilege of witnessing. God shut down their plans for a building program, however, effectively saying, "No, you have to get it right. We're not here to erect structures. We are here to experience the supernatural and natural realms."

The disciples eventually got it. Peter learned about angels when one hit him on the shoulder, woke him up and led him from prison the night before he was to be executed. The angel said: "Peter, go through those gates. Go to this house. They are praying for you."

He finally came to his senses—he thought he was dreaming—and knocked on the door. A servant girl opened the door, slammed it in his face and ran to tell her the others that Peter was at the door. "It cannot be Peter," they said. "We are praying for him; he is in jail. He can't be here, released... although that's what we are praying for. It must be his angel." (ref. Acts 12:5-19)

Well, it was Peter all right, released by the power of God working simultaneously in the natural and supernatural realms.

We have a right to these two realms in the Kingdom. There is the supra, which is above the natural *in authority*—that contains God's unseen realm. The natural is our seen realm. In creating the invisible world (supernatural), this act of creation gave us the concepts of ruler and rulership. God created us so we could do in this realm what he does in his realm.

What is another word for ruler? It is King. What did God call the invisible realm? He called it his domain; he called it heaven. That is his; that is where he operates. Remember, every time we look at Jesus talking about the Father to people, he felt the need to give them Father's geographical location. He would say, "Our Father in heaven, your Father in heaven." Unless he was talking to the Pharisees and the scribes, then he would say: "Your father, the devil." He never said: "Your father in hell." That was because the devil had not faced final judgment yet.

God operates in this unseen realm called heaven. The Bible says that God created the heavens for himself, and he created the earth for the sons of men. He created the earth for you and me to rule in. God rules in the invisible, the unseen, and gives us the responsibility to rule the seen (ref. Psalm 8). At the beginning of all things created, the first kingdom was called the invisible Kingdom of God, the invisible influence of God, the Kingdom of Heaven.

The concept of kingdom is essential, necessary, required, and imperative to understand, appreciate and comprehend the purpose, intent, goal and objectives of God and mankind's relationship to him and the creation. God is showing us our relationship is to him and to creation. Religion says, "Your relationship is to God, but at best he is an absentee dad. Because he is way out there and he left you here, but one day he is going to come home and get you and take you back to his house."

That is the epitome of false doctrine. God is not an absentee Dad. He is:

A very present help in trouble.

Psalm 46:1 KJV

He will never leave you nor forsake you.

Deuteronomy 31:6 NIV

I have never seen the righteous forsaken or their children begging bread.

Psalm 37:25

David was a kingdom man. Religion has taught us that God is way out there in another realm, but Hebrew culture teaches us that these realms intertwine with one another and that we can step into the Father's presence in that throne room any time we desire. It can be as real as this right here.

The writers of the Bible describe many supernatural experiences—times when the reality of the "supra" or the supernatural invaded the realm of the natural. One of these is the great cloud of witnesses described in Hebrews 11 and 12. These are heroes of the faith who see our progress and urge us on.

I have seen into the cloud of witnesses many times. We have seen some of them in our meetings. We have even seen significant people who I thought might not have made it to heaven show up in the cloud of witnesses. Others on our team have seen them as well. Often, we are standing next to one another and saying, "This is what I am seeing," and we are seeing the exact same thing. It is as real as anyone I see in the natural.

This is only possible if we are intertwined with the natural and supernatural. We operate from the same place that Jesus operates from. We are able to operate in both realms simultaneously because that is kingdom. Religion cannot do that. Kingdom does it all the time:

> *And raised us up with Him, and seated us with Him in the heavenly places in Christ Jesus.*

> Ephesians 2:6

ADOPTION

We have been given *radah*, kingdom, rulership over all of the earth. The Bible tells us in the Book of Romans:

> *For we know that the whole creation groans and suffers the pains of childbirth together until now.*

> Romans 8:22

The earth is crying out for us to step out of religion and get back in the kingdom of God so the earth can begin to do what it was designed to do. The earth cannot function as designed as long as we are tilling it with our hands. It needs to respond to kingdom words of sons and daughters. Jesus did everything as a man who walked in the natural and the supernatural. So can we. So *must* we!

For all who are being led by the Spirit of God, these are sons of God. For you have not received a spirit of slavery leading to fear again, but you have received a spirit of adoption as sons and daughters *by which we cry out, "Abba! Father!"*

Romans 8:14-15

The writer here is Paul, and the immediate recipient is the Roman church. The meaning in their culture is that Christianity is not some new kind of religion. The Roman church mostly came out of pagan religion. This is the meaning behind saying they have not received a spirit of slavery leading to fear but have received a spirit of adoption.

Paul is telling these converted pagans that the Holy Spirit of God testifies with their spirit that they are the children of God. They are grafted into a new and everlasting family through a spiritual connection.

On a broader scale—and this is why we have the Bible—Paul's words are reminding each of us of where we come from. The stories and testimonies of the Bible have been preserved by God to do just that—assert and affirm our place in him...in his kingdom. The book of Revelation says that we overcome by the blood of the lamb and the word of our testimony (ref. Revelation 12:11). Considering the power of testimony, Paul further says that Holy Spirit himself is testifying to us.

The Spirit Himself testifies with our spirit that we are children of God, and if children, heirs also, heirs of God and fellow heirs with Christ, if indeed we suffer with Him so that we may also be glorified with Him.

Romans 8:16-17

Now, Paul was writing about adoption as understood by the culture of the Galatians at that time. Here's what that looked like.

What I am saying is that as long as an heir is underage, he is no different from a slave, although he owns the whole estate. The heir is subject to guardians and trustees until the time set by his father. So also, when we were underage, we were in slavery under the elemental spiritual forces of the world. But when the set time had fully come, God sent his Son, born of a woman, born under the law, to redeem those under the law, that we might receive adoption to sonship. Because you are his sons, God sent the Spirit of his Son into our hearts, the Spirit who calls out, "Abba, Father." So you are no longer a slave, but God's child; and since you are his child, God has made you also an heir.

Galatians 4:1-7

When the father sees that we have matured to a son, he starts the adoption process. He calls the city together. He calls his household— brothers and sisters, servants, everybody in the house, everyone connected with him. Merchants are invited to the adoption, and they all come to watch the father adopt the son. This is how God does it. He brings the son up in front of all of those he has invited. He puts his arm around his son and pulls him in tight to himself. That is the adoption process. He pulls him in close to where there is no space between them. He declares, "Today, this is my son. I present him to you. When you see him coming, you see me coming. When he asks for something from your business in my name, he is asking as if it is me asking of you. He has come to a place of maturity that I can trust him with the expansion of the family business."

The father then gives his son a ring, a robe and he puts new shoes on his feet.

Glory to God! The father says: "Now, my son is no longer a child. He is a son and he now is a partner in the family business. You see him, you see me, end of story. If he wants to buy something, he has a ring to purchase it, and it's on my credit. It is on my charge. It is because of who I am, and now who my son is. With the ring he is able to purchase."

That was adoption in Roman culture. It closely parallels adoption by our heavenly Father as well.

The Spirit himself testifies with our spirit that we are the children of God. He reminds us of who we are because it's easy to get caught up in the identity the world offers. We are not Christians in the religious sense. We are sons and daughters of God in the kingdom sense. We have a blood relationship with the Father—the blood of Jesus. The term *adoption* in Romans 8 and Galatians 4 does not mean we were previously homeless, parentless or without an inheritance. Adoption meant something different in Roman culture. In that culture, a father actually adopted his own son when he reached maturity. Before adoption, the child was considered immature, possessing the status of an orphan or a slave, having nothing in the way of authority. Paul refers to this in Galatians.

> *As long as the heir is a child, he does not differ at all from a slave, although he is owner of everything:*

Galatians 4:1

The term *child* means "immature." It is drawn from the root word *orphan.* As long as someone thinks like an orphan, they are no different than a slave. Even though they are the future owner of everything, they are ruled by governors and managers until the date for adoption set by the father.

Likewise, when we come to the Lord, we often come into the kingdom possessing an orphan heart. We are newly minted believers but with childish ways. We have immature hearts, all-about-me hearts. We fall easily into traps.

- Why wasn't I promoted when they were promoted?
- I am more gifted than they are.
- Why does she let them sing and not me?
- It's because she knows I am a better singer than her.
- My anointing is greater than theirs; why don't I get to speak?

That is an orphan's heart. It's an independent heart to a fault. It says, "I do not need anybody to oversee me or cover me in ministry because I am called to this. I am an apostle myself. Why do I need to be tied to another apostle's heart?"

You need to be tied to another apostle's heart because you are... an orphan!

In the culture of the Galatian church, the father watched his children and determined the right date to set for the son's adoption. This has parallels in the kingdom as well. Father God watches us grow out of our orphan heart and into the heart of a son.

A son in Roman culture was one who participated in the father's business. Unlike our modern times, Roman sons did not go off to college to learn. They were never asked what they wanted to be when they grow up. That question was irrelevant; if your father was a blacksmith, you were going to be a blacksmith. If your father was a philosopher, you would be a philosopher. If your father was a soldier, you would be a soldier. If your father was a king, you would be a king.

Likewise, in the kingdom definition, the answer to "What are you going to be when you grow up?" is easy. "Your Father is the King. You will be a king. Any more questions?"

In Galatians 4, Paul is telling us the Father is watching us grow out of our orphan heart. We are given a governor and a tutor—managers who helps us learn and grow into mature sonship. In our case, our governor is Holy Spirit. Our tutor is the fivefold ministry God puts in our lives to equip us to do what he has called us to do.

> *For you have not received a spirit of slavery leading to fear again, but you have received a spirit of adoption as sons and daughters by which we cry out, "Abba! Father!"*

Romans 8:15

As we grow, a process called *adoption* takes place in which we mature into the fullness of sonship. Note that this doesn't mean complete maturity. When we are born again, we are children of God. Through the spirit of adoption, however, we grow into sonship— mature sons and daughters of God.

Again, *child* means "orphan" in Galatians—one of immature character. The father watches that child, waiting until he's matured, grown enough to begin assuming responsibility. Note that in the culture of the day, even after the event called adoption, the son was not ready to assume control of everything. Rather, the son was still being groomed.

In today's vernacular, it'd be like your dad calling together the shop employees and announcing: "OK, everybody. I'm getting too old to run this place by myself. Greg is now in charge. He's gonna make mistakes. He'll need your help. But he's the first guy you go to for a decision. I'll be around, but Greg is now the designated heir. He has the keys to the building. He speaks for me. Greg's word is my word. And if he messes up, I'll deal with him."

Sonship is a process. Maturation is process. Yes, you're a son or daughter in the sense of being one of the family of God, but you are not entrusted with everything. We read in John 1:9-13:

This was the true Light [Jesus] that, coming into the world, enlightens every person. He was in the world, and the world came into being through Him, and yet the world did not know Him. He came to His own, and His own people did not accept Him. But as many as received Him, to them He gave the right to become children of God, to those who believe in His name, who were born, not of blood, nor of the will of the flesh, nor of the will of a man, but of God.

Notice the offer of God to as many as received Jesus: "the right to become the children of God." That identifies a process, one which starts when we are born again, and it proceeds through maturity.

At age 12, Jesus addressed his harried parents who, after three days of frantic searching, found him debating religious scholars in the Jerusalem temple:

When Joseph and Mary saw Him [Jesus], they were bewildered; and His mother said to Him, "Son, why have You treated us this way? Behold, Your father and I have been anxiously looking for You!"

And He said to them, "Why is it that you were looking for Me? Did you not know that I had to be in My Father's house?"

But they did not understand what he was saying to them.

Luke 2:48-50

His parents didn't get it, at least not fully. To them, Jesus was still their son, the little boy they raised from birth. That's who he was to God as well—still the son of God, but with some more growing to do. Jesus must have sensed this as well. Rather than turn from his parents, he submitted to them, his tutors and governors in this life:

> *Then he went down to Nazareth with them and was obedient to them. But his mother treasured all these things in her heart. And Jesus grew in wisdom and stature, and in favor with God and man.*

Luke 2:51-53

Jesus "grew in wisdom and stature." That implies that he was not done growing yet. Indeed, it was not until his baptism at age 30 that the Father launched him into the family business. Not Joseph's carpentry business, but a different kind of business. No longer building houses, but building a kingdom.

> *As soon as Jesus was baptized, he went up out of the water. At that moment heaven was opened, and he saw the Spirit of God descending like a dove and alighting on him. And a voice from heaven said, "This is my Son, whom I love; with him I am well pleased.*

Matthew 3:16-17

God made a public declaration of adoption. Jesus was activated to sonship and walked for three years in ministry and changed the world forever. Jesus was bringing a family business back into order, though not in a religious sense. The family business was kingdom.

The Father watches us grow; he teaches us to leave our orphan's heart. As we mature, we find that life is no longer about us. It's not even about the Father, but about his business.

HEIR

Being an heir of God's does not mean that God has to die to give us stuff. That is Western thinking. Hebrew-Roman thinking is different. The reason the prodigal son in Luke 15 could demand his inheritance and squander it was because there were two sons, so the inheritance was divided evenly between them with the oldest son having the opportunity to keep the family homestead.

The second son got an equal inheritance, and he could go do whatever he wanted to do anywhere. The oldest son in that story never intended to leave home because he knew that was where he would operate from. The second son said: "I want mine and I want to go now." So they could get it anytime if they wanted it after being recognized as mature.

Now, if there were more than two sons, the oldest son got everything and distributed it among the other sons. Fortunately, God does not have multiple sons. He has one. Yes, we are sons as well (even the daughters are sons), but we are one in Christ.

> *For if by the offense of the one, death reigned through the one, much more will those who receive the abundance of grace and of the gift of righteousness reign in life through the One, Jesus Christ.*

> Romans 5:17

Good news. We are not struggling on our own. We are the firstborn because we are *in* the firstborn. We reign through the firstborn. We have had the idea that Jesus is our older brother. That is not accurate. There is only one son—that son includes us in him. So, we have an inheritance. We are fellow heirs with Christ. If indeed we suffer with him, we do so that we may also be glorified with him:

> *For I consider that the sufferings of this present time are not worthy to be compared with the glory that is to be revealed to us.*

> Romans 8:18

CREATION'S YEARNING

The anxious longing of creation waits eagerly for the revealing of the sons of God:

For the creation was subjected to futility, not willingly, but because of Him who subjected it, in hope that the creation itself also will be set free from its slavery to corruption into the freedom of the glory of the children of God.

For we know that the whole creation groans and suffers the pains of childbirth together until now. And not only that, but also we ourselves, having the first fruits of the Spirit, even we ourselves groan within ourselves, waiting eagerly for our adoption as sons and daughters, the redemption of our body. For in hope we have been saved, but hope that is seen is not hope; for who hopes for what he already sees? But if we hope for what we do not see, through perseverance we wait eagerly for it.

Romans 8:19-25

For the creation was subjected to futility not willingly but because of Adam. If creation itself will also be set free from its slavery to corruption into freedom of the glory, whose glory will that be? Our glory.

Paul refers to having the first fruits of this Spirit, but understand that Paul, in this culture, was saying they were the first fruits. Today, we have opportunity to live more. We are groaning within ourselves. We wait eagerly for our adoption as sons, the redemption of our body and all of creation. From Romans 8:26-27:

Now in the same way the Spirit also helps our weakness; for we do not know what to pray for as we should, but the Spirit Himself intercedes for us with groanings too deep for words; and He who searches the hearts knows what the mind of the Spirit is, because He intercedes for the saints according to the will of God.

HOLY SPIRIT INTERCEDES

The Spirit intercedes for the saints according to the will of God. This is the governor in us. We do not know how to pray, so he prays through us in our native dialect. Your native dialect is a heavenly language called tongues. Groanings, travail, intercession are expressions of our native dialect. The Bible talks about two languages that are spoken in our kingdom nation. It is our heavenly language and the language of angels: a different dialect.

The earth is groaning. The earth is in labor pains for you and I to come into who God has called us to be—mature adopted sons and daughters of God. Jesus is our example. Everything he did, he did as man. He did nothing in the earth as a deity. Jesus had a way with creation as man.

CREATION'S RESPONSE

In Mark 4, Jesus was taking a nap in the bottom of a boat while a storm raged all around. His panicked disciples woke him up and said, "Teacher, do you not care that we are perishing?"

So Jesus got up and rebuked the wind and said to the sea, "Hush, be still." And the wind died down and it became perfectly calm. Then he turned to his disciples, the people he was training to advance the kingdom over the earth after he departed. "Why are you afraid? Do you still have no faith?"

In essence, Jesus was saying: "I was sleeping well. Why did you wake me up? You could have taken care of this yourselves!"

The disciples looked at each other and said, "Who, then, is this, that even the wind and the sea obey him?"

The man was Jesus, and he was able to govern with his words, not his hands. He was a kingdom man.

WALKING ON WATER

In Matthew 14, Jesus and his disciples had finished feeding the 5,000, and he told his disciples to take a boat to the other side of the sea while he went up on a mountain by himself to pray. Hours later, a storm arose and in the fourth watch, Jesus came walking on the water to where his disciples were battling the waves as they tried to reach shore.

How did this happen? The instant Jesus put his foot on the water, the molecules changed. Creation changed to support him because he had a destination. Today, we look at this famous occurrence and say: "Oh, that was just a supernatural thing that only Jesus could do."

No, it wasn't. This was not some cool trick that Jesus saw the Father do in Heaven. It was an example of Jesus governing as a Son of God. He stepped out on the water and walked as if it was solid ground. The water obeyed Him. It responded to him as a Son of God. His disciples, unfortunately, slipped back into their superstitions when they saw Jesus, crying out: "It is a ghost!"

Only Peter was feeling brave. "Lord, if it is you, command me to come to you on the water."

"Come!" said Jesus.

Peter left the boat and the water changed for him as well. He walked on the water just as Jesus was doing... until he got scared and began to sink. That's when Jesus reached out and took hold of him.

Now, what we do not preach too often about this story, unless you are a kingdom person, is what happened next. Jesus reached down and picked up Peter, but the Bible does not say that Peter was carried by Jesus. It does not say Jesus slung him over his shoulder and hauled him to safety. No. The implication is that they walked back to the boat together. The sea responded to a mature Son and a maturing son. Hallelujah!

FIG TREE

In Mark 11, Jesus and his disciples were walking one day and Jesus was hungry. He passed a fig tree and the Bible says distinctly that Jesus wanted a fig, but the tree had no figs on it because it was out of season. So, it was not expected to have a fig on it in the natural. Jesus walked by and He said: "May no one ever eat fruit from you again!"

Now people like to take that fig tree and make it Israel and throw the interpretation into the future as some kind of prophetic word. But actually, it was a fig tree from which Jesus wanted a fig. It's that simple. The fig tree did not respond to him as the Son of God and so, Jesus essentially said: "You will not produce figs any longer because you did not respond to my voice."

God expects things to produce for him, even if they are out of season. The Word tells us to be ready in season and out of season:

I solemnly exhort you in the presence of God and of Christ Jesus, who is to judge the living and the dead, and by His appearing and His kingdom: preach the word; be ready in season and out of season; correct, rebuke, and exhort, with great patience and instruction.

2 Timothy 4:1-2

What is "out of season"? Like, I can't shoot a buck in July? No. It means:

- I'm tired, so I'm just going to go home to bed.
- I don't feel like coming tonight.
- These people are hard-headed. Lord, they are not going to get the message.
- Lord, I am not going to do all that. What's it going to be?
- Why should we go into that city and pray?

Yes, we all get tired, discouraged, even a little bored. But God expects fruit in season and out of season. It is time for the earth to respond to the mature sons of God, in season and out of season.

RESTORED

Jesus came to model restoration and redemption. Everything God does is redemptive in its nature. Even his judgment is redemptive in nature. God is not a plan B God. He is a plan A God. When he restored us, he did not leave us hanging until he could come rapture us out of here. Through Jesus Christ, he put us back into the original intent of his heart—the same place Adam was in. He told us to do the same thing he had told Adam to do.

When I was a young man (back in my hair days), I was at a tent meeting in Tupelo, Mississippi, at the church where I got filled with the Spirit. Pastor Cecil Pumphrey had a tent out front and he loved tents. We had meetings that went for weeks and weeks.

One day, a bunch of us were standing outside and a tornado was approaching. The wind began thrusting the tent ceiling up and down. The tiedown ropes came loose and the tent was in danger of flying away.

Pastor Cecil hollered: "Boys, grab a rope."

I'm thinking: *No, let us go inside and let this tent fend for itself.*

But Pastor Cecil was intent on saving his tent.

"Grab a rope!"

So we each grabbed a rope and now we were being yanked off our feet as that tent was blowing up and down. (This was in my 165-pound days. Today, I could have anchored the whole thing.)

We could see the funnel cloud approaching. We were holding onto the ropes for dear life. I couldn't tell who was winning—us or the tornado. But we were spending more time bouncing into the air than on the ground. What was the sense in saving this hunk of canvas when a perfectly sound brick structure was nearby and calling our names?

Just when it looked as though we were scheduled for an early departure from this earth, something happened that changed my life forever. Pastor Cecil turned to the howling tornado, stuck his finger in the air and yelled: "In the name of Jesus, I command you to disappear!"

And it went *poof!* Clouds dissipated and the wind calmed!

Oh, thank you, Jesus.

He spoke to the storm and it disappeared. *Jesus 1. Storm 0.*

Years later, Joan and I were home when a tornado appeared. We stood in the doorway and began to pray, declaring: "Tornado, you will not touch our house. You will not! You will go around our house."

And that's exactly what it did.

When we went out the next morning to inspect the debris, the neighbor was on his porch and said: "Greg, you will not believe what happened."

"Try me," I said.

"That tornado jumped your house last night."

It jumped our house, hit our neighbor's barn and tore it down. I don't know if the neighbor didn't have faith or what, but he lost the barn. We kept our house.

We have seen things like that so many times in our life. Creation responds to our voice. You need to expect that. You need to have a wisdom in those places, too. Remember Paul got on the boat headed to Rome and he said, "Guys, let's not go," (ref. Acts 27).

"No, you are going. We are going in this thing," they said.

And then the storm came and the angel said, "Paul, your boat is going to bust up, but nobody is going to lose their life."

That is also power over a storm.

Later, Paul was gathering firewood and a snake bit him. He shook it off into the fire. Now the snake bite should have killed him, but it never affected him, and the natives thought Paul was a god (ref. Acts 28).

Of course, some would say: "Well, if it was really God, Paul should never have gotten bit by the snake in the first place."

Not so. Only after Paul was bit did the natives pay attention to him. They would never have thought he was a god if he had not been bit. It changed their entire perspective.

People need to hear you, they do not just need to hear me. You need to get this in you and go preach it, teach it, and share it with everybody that you can. Write books on it, do movies about it. Whatever you want to do, do it, but get the gospel of the Kingdom out.

Amen.

12

Conclusion

THROUGHOUT THIS STUDY, we have focused on the Kingdom of God—a term used often in Christianity but not well understood. I have sought to present the Kingdom of God as Jesus meant it. In so doing, I have probably upended many cherished notions and entrenched concepts. So be it. We are in a revolution.

As we discussed, Jesus' purpose on the earth was not to get people saved from hell. He never preached a salvation message—not one! Rather, he preached the Kingdom of God. Nowhere in the gospels do we find Jesus preaching any other message but kingdom; not prosperity, nor deliverance, nor healing, nor salvation. He preached the gospel of the kingdom, and when he did, all of those other things— prosperity, deliverance, healing, salvation and more—manifested in the process. He did not preach these things; he lived them.

This might be a good time to say: "Go and do likewise."

Family, this is so fundamental, I have to repeat it. Jesus did not come to earth to get people saved in the conventional sense of salvation. He came to build his ekklesia—his church, his government. The concept of a personal relationship with Jesus is great, but it is incomplete. Salvation, as Jesus embodied it, is both personal and kingdom, inward and outward.

Recall Jesus' words from the sermon on the mount: "Blessed are the peacemakers." Interesting term: peacemaker. It means more than "one who is at peace." It refers to one who makes peace; one who is a source of peace.

We know that Jesus came to make peace between us and the Father. But do we realize that peace is not the end goal? The end goal, as Jesus espoused on the famous mount, is to be a source of peace—to give. It is the outward flow that Jesus spoke of when he said,

The one who believes in me, as the Scripture said, 'From his innermost being will flow rivers of living water'"

John 7:38

The Kingdom of God is not a dwelling place. It is not simply our habitation, our refuge, our hiding place, safely tucked away until Jesus returns and sets all to right in this wicked world. Rather, it is the place from which we rule, reign, occupy, and proliferate. We are not called to be inert. We are called as kings. Kings are not passive; at least not for long. Passive kings soon find themselves dethroned. King David fell into deep sin when his army was in the field and he remained ensconced in his palace. Moses, safe in the palace of Pharoah, was driven out before he could be of use to God.

Christianity is not for the timid or the entitled. Yes, we dance around at our gatherings, cheering all that God has given us, but do we really understand what we are celebrating? God has not merely given us the kingdom. He has called us to operate in the kingdom.

The differences are stark.

Religion will tell you to receive, to hold the ground, to stay faithful 'till the end. But that is not the entire Kingdom message Jesus preached. If I have to exhort you every week to stay the course, would that not indicate that I don't have much to offer...other than the promise of better things to come? There comes a point where a promise, like a fragrant blossom, must give way to real fruit. To do so, we must understand the business we are in. We are in the business of the Kingdom of God, not religion.

Jesus did not come to restore the Jewish religion, nor did he come to establish a new religion in his name. He came to give us a new government under his authority, one that works, one that requires our participation. Jesus redeemed the Kingdom of God on earth.

Ekklesia is not a religious word; it is a governmental word. Jesus' intention was never for us to focus on heaven, but to focus on changing the culture of the colony of earth to mirror heaven. We are not being prepared to enter heaven. That is religion. Rather, we are preparing the earth to receive heaven. That is kingdom.

We have to get out of our religious structures—our physical boxes of pews, stained glass and steeples. These serve a purpose, but their purpose is not for us to serve them. We have to get out of our religious mindsets as well. Yes, an inferior understanding of kingdom is better than no understanding of kingdom, but when true kingdom is realized, we must release our old understanding and embrace the new understanding. That is why God is revealing what he did 2,000 years ago. It's not a mystery; it's not a message written in the dark for a select few. It has been hiding in plain sight for centuries. God is moving, yet he will not do what he intends on the earth through a religious mindset that produces disorder. He is preparing us to receive him.

When Adam fell, he did not lose a religion. He lost a kingdom. He lost rulership. He lost *radah*. And the enemy claimed all that was lost.

Jesus came to restore what Adam lost. As believers in Jesus, we are kings. We go forth as kings. We fight like kings. Our weapons are declarations, decrees and prophetic words that release the army of God, which is the angelic host. The enemy should see kings on the battlefield, not a sea of foot soldiers, sergeants, lieutenants and a few generals, but kings united in releasing the decrees of the Lord and reaping the spoils of battle.

We have a heavenly responsibility to engage the country we live in. Our vote is our voice; it is heard when we hold accountable those who are in office. We can fill our heads with knowledge and still make no difference in the world. To be effective for the kingdom, knowledge has to be activated by purpose and passion for our assignment.

What does God's kingdom look like? How does it play out in our lives? Do we walk about wearing gold crowns and speaking in Elizabethan English? "Thou, thus, thine..." We could do that, but we'd be declared nuts, and I'd have to agree.

The fact is, we all work our jobs. Even preachers work. (Try it sometime, if you think otherwise.) As Christians, however, we work from a kingdom perspective. We are not toiling at just any business. We are working our Father's business. Even as we go through life in business, ministry, arts, entertainment, truck driving, teaching, construction or banking, our lives are rooted in kingdom purpose because God inhabits the lives of his people. As such, we release worship and praise to God, and everybody around us notices.

Recall our self-examination.

- Why am I here?
- Why am I in this business?
- Why am I in this branch of business?
- Why am I in this city with this business?
- Why have I birthed a business in this city?
- What is God's heart for this place in which he has placed me?

As you search out these things in prayer, the Father will download your purpose, and you will begin to understand the reason for being where you are.

As believers in Christ, we are called to key environments, not to conform them but to transform them. The difference is direction and effectiveness. Conformity comes from the outside. It is the application of external pressure, rooted in coercion and often unpleasant. Transformation, however, comes from the inside. It is the natural outcome of an internal condition. That's how kingdom grows.

Are you looking for the Kingdom of God? Where to serve? Where to operate from? My friends, look no further.

The kingdom of God is not coming with signs that can be observed; nor will they say, "Look, here it is!" or, "There it is!" For behold, the kingdom of God is in your midst.

Luke 17:20-21

You can't escape it. The Kingdom of God is in you; you are in the Kingdom of God. You are of the family of God, a son or daughter of God, an heir to the kingdom. The transformation has begun...within you and beyond you. You know that stirring you feel? That nudge, that angst, that yearning for something better for you and the world? That's the kingdom rising up and coming forth. That's your kingship calling you. It's your destiny to possess all that Adam lost and to rule as man was intended, through our lives, our families, our businesses. We are to rule as Jesus leads.

Jesus was activated to sonship at his baptism. He walked for three years in ministry and changed the world. Jesus brought the family business back into order, yet not in a religious sense. The family business was kingdom. We are now in the kingdom.

The Father nurturers us. He weans us from our orphan's heart. As we mature, we discover that life is no longer about us. It's not even about the Father, but about his business.

It is my prayer that you would receive and learn to operate in God's kingdom. There is no greater purpose in life.

PRAYER

Father, I pray that you would empower me by Holy Spirit to shift from a religious mindset, which has held me back from walking in the fullness as a son who is partnering with you, to a mindset that aligns me more and more with your Kingdom. Give me the revelation needed to change the way I relate to the world, read your Word, view myself and expand your kingdom. Father, bring your church, your Ekklesia, into her full kingdom purpose. In Jesus Name!

DECREE

I decree that I am returning to God's original intent for me as a son, partnering with God in his kingdom.

I decree that I am shifting out of the chains of religion NOW!

I decree that I am finding my place within the Ekklesia for Kingdom expansion!

In Jesus Name!

About the Author

GREG HOOD WAS BORN AND RAISED IN AMORY, MISSISSIPPI, and has been in ministry for over 36 years. He is the President and Founder of Greg Hood Ministries, The Network of Five-Fold Ministers and Churches, as well as Kingdom University, all are based in the United States of America.

Greg apostolically leads many leaders and churches around the globe. He is a planter of apostolic centers and has pioneered several apostolic centers within the United States and in other parts of the globe. Greg travels extensively, empowering believers for the passionate pursuit of their God-given mandate, resulting in personal and societal transformation. His greatest passion is to see the Body of Christ come to its fullness within the Kingdom of God. Greg is driven with great passion to speak into those who are called into leadership to the Church, Government, and the Marketplace. He burns to see people become who God has fashioned them to be.

Greg and his wife, Joan, have been married for 25 years. After finishing a 10-year assignment in Hawaii, in 2020 the Hood's moved their ministry headquarters to Amory, Mississippi where it still resides.

Previous Work

Praise for *Rebuilding the Broken Altar – Awakening Out of Chaos.*

This book is as loaded with keen insight and Spirit-inspired revelation as any you will find. You would be hard pressed to find a book more timely and more relevant for the Church and the nations—especially America—than Rebuilding the Broken Altar. Sadly, many books simply restate others' teachings, simply coloring them with a different spin. However, it is refreshing when I read a book that feeds me new thoughts and information. Simply stated, I was more than entertained and inspired by Greg's book—I learned a lot!

Dr. Dutch Sheets, Dutch Sheets Ministries and Give Him 15 daily prayer and decrees.
Bestselling author of: *Authority in Prayer, An Appeal to Heaven, Intercessory Prayer*

If there was ever a time when a people needed to return to the Lord it is now. In his book "Rebuilding the Broken Altar" Greg Hood gives insight to the necessary process of recovering ourselves from the snare of the devil and experiencing the blessing of God again as a people. I would encourage, as you read to allow the Holy Spirit to stir your heart again with His passion for us individually and as a nation.

Robert Henderson
Best Selling Author of *The Courts of Heaven Series*

In *Rebuilding the Broken Altar*, Greg Hood presents a masterpiece of hope for the future of the church, for America and for nations crying out for a move of God. He carefully, biblically and prophetically lays out a blueprint for revival that every leader and believer alike can work with to shift culture and engage the spiritual atmosphere to bring change. The word studies bring incredible insight and reveal the important elements necessary for rebuilding the altar of the Lord which has been broken down in both the church and in society in order to see an unprecedented outpouring from heaven, for harvest and transformation.

Dr. Jane Hamon, Vision Church @ Christian International
Author of: *Dreams and Visions, The Deborah Company, The Cyrus Decree, Discernment*

My friend Greg Hood is known as hard-hitting, straight-shooting and uncompromising in his preaching. His writing is even more so! I love the way he boldly challenges us to break free from old religious mindsets so that we can embrace God's kingdom plans. In his new book *Rebuilding the Broken Altar*, Greg gives us a clear vision of a restored church. With rich insights about the twelve tribes of Israel, he takes us on a journey toward the restoration of New Testament faith. You will be challenged and inspired!

J. Lee Grady, Author and Director of The Mordecai Project

Dr. Greg Hood helps us to understand the meaning of the time and grasp the seismic impact of the altar. I have had the privilege of Greg's friendship and the blessings of his clear prophetic voices. I praise the Lord Jesus for enabling him to write this valuable book.

Tamrat Layne, Former Prime Minister, Ethiopia

The bottom-line message of this book, God is not finished with you or America, but the church and some pastors and some of us in government need to get our stones together.

Rep. Gene Ward, PhD, Hawai'i House of Representatives

Made in United States
Orlando, FL
09 June 2023

33964308R00113